VOLUME I

Writer's
BANE
Write, Revise, Publish, & Repeat

Research

VOLUME I

Writer's BANE

Write, Revise, Publish, & Repeat

Research

VALERIE WILLIS

4 Horsemen
Publications, Inc.

4 Horsemen
Publications, Inc.

4 Horsemen Publications, Inc.
1497 Main St. Suite 169
Dunedin, FL 34698
4horsemenpublications.com
info@4horsemenpublications.com

Cover & Typesetting by Battle Goddess Productions
Editor J.M. Paquette

Paperback ISBN-13: 978-1-64450-107-8

DISCLAIMER

This book is for a wide range of writers and authors. There will be information from all levels of writing within to help everyone from aspiring to veteran authors. You will find insight on a variety of aspects that may provide support where needed. Other chapters may not be relevant to the choices you make, such as choosing a publishing path which will split between the many paths, so the writer can see the differences, evaluate the expectations, and make an informed decision. Unfortunately, the world of writers and publishing, especially self-publishing or independent publishing, changes every three to six months. At the release of this book, I aimed to be as relevant as possible to the current trends, statistics, and information available during the production of this all-inclusive guide on writing, editing, revising, formatting, publishing, and more.

In short, it is important you realize not all the content may be agreeable, set in stone, or the preferred standard. This is a based on the viewpoint from me, a fellow author, writer, and creative, who aims to do what she can to provide a variety of examples from all genres, but you should know my forte is in fantasy, paranormal, romance, and mythology remakes. Regardless, there should be enough information and content to meet a writer's needs, and you are encouraged to use this as a toolbox. Pick out the tools that best fit you and your journey and use them to write, polish, and publish your book.

WHAT IS THE WRITER'S BANE?

> **bane** /bān/ *noun*
>
> a cause of great distress or annoyance.
> *"The bane of the decorator is the long, narrow hall."*
>
> **Similar:** scourge, ruin, death, plague, ruination, destruction, torment, torture, menace, suffering, pain, distress, hardship, cross to bear, burden, thorn in one's flesh/side, bitter pill, affliction, calamity, despair, trouble, misery, woe, tribulation, misfortune, nuisance, pest, headache, trial, blight, curse, nightmare
>
> **ARCHAIC:** *something, typically poison, that causes death.*
>
> *Definition from Oxford Languages*

A bane or curse: to have a story, a desire to share it, and the task of polishing it for public consumption, facing the highs and lows of agents and publishers, traversing editors and feedback, and creating a book as the end result. It's a curse—a wonderful one—that haunts every waking and slumbering minute of a writer's life. A desire to see a story from start to finish is needed to quell it, even if it's for a mere breath of one's time on this earth.

The Writer's Bane will test your resolve, time and time again.

Search Google and you find the definition of *bane*:

A cause of great distress or annoyance

Well, the Writer's Bane is exactly that. We often find ourselves in distress or annoyed with some part of the process. Whether we are fighting writer's block to trying to figure out how to Track Changes in Word, we all have our lists of issues during our start to finish process on a book.

It doesn't matter if you are publishing your first novel or the thirty-millionth novel, each book or story tends to create its own batch of issues. Just look at this sentence:

"The bane of the [writer] is the long, narrow hall."

This is true on so many levels. You will find yourself in narrow halls where restrictions will force you to move in one or a limited choice of direction. Whether it is writing within the expectations of a genre, romance versus horror, or following the industry standards in writing, editing, and publishing, this cursed hallway gets longer and narrower. In fact, it can be a creative killer if you're not prepared. Be sure to arm yourself properly.

The Writer's Bane is a toolbox. *Your toolbox.* A suitcase to hold onto as you traverse one hall and turn down the next one of your choosing. Down these halls, you find the doors labelled with warnings, *bane's* many synonyms:

What is the Writer's Bane?

*Scourge. Ruin. Death.
Plague. Ruination.
Destruction.*

You will counter each of these on some level. Worst, you may feel these about your work, the process, or yourself. We call this *imposter syndrome* when we doubt the idea that we can be the writer and author we already have become. Just remember and know that only you can tell and write your story. There will be a good amount of blood, sweat, and tears shed in each hall you travel down. Some of these parts will *plague* you, others will feel like a slow *death*, and other times you will feel as if you've brought the whole project to *ruin*.

It's okay. We live through this.

Remember you're cursed but still fighting and have a lucky charm (this book). Use the tools to destroy the *scourge* with your confidence and resilience. The only person who can make this story idea turn itself into a book is YOU. No one else. It's an age-old fact and has been this way since the days of Charles Dickens selling the *Christmas Carol*. He resisted! How? By performing live readings because he had to "self-publish" after being turned down by publishers. Only the writer can overcome and cure the curse, no matter what form it takes.

This book is designed to be a lucky charm to combat your curse, this curse, and more importantly, *our* curse as writers. This covers front to back, start to finish, the process, thoughts, knowledge, and experiences collected by author Valerie Willis. A lot of it isn't just for the publishing industry or writers but branches into the realm of game development and graphic design. It may not have a cure for every part of your curse, but it aims to provide some relief and keep you moving forward.

*ARCHAIC: something,
typically poison, that
causes death.*

The Writer's Bane is poison. Our curse is something to build immunity to, much like a real poison. Royalty in the past such as young princes and princesses often died trying to build immunity to poisons. As a warning, your bane may kill your desire to be a writer or author. You will need to develop a thick skin, be stubborn and fight hard, and every time you fall, wipe the mud from your face and hop back on that bucking bull or bronco. There will be bumps, bruises, scrapes, and even times where you feel beyond broken. I can promise that you aren't the first to feel this way or walk these halls.

This is the Writer's Bane.

You must know this going in: find a support group of fellow writers. We all have this curse, this desire to create and tell a story, to see it made into something tangible and let it fly out into the open skies like so many creations before it. Fellow writers will be able to give you a hand through those tighter hallways where the walls squeeze you until you no longer can move. Combined with this tome of advice, other writers can pull you through, taking down some walls, unlocking some doors, and widening some halls that seemed impassible.

*"Welcome
to the
writing tribe."*

WORDS OF ENCOURAGEMENT

Moral of the story, if you read who I am, is NEVER GIVE UP. No matter how ugly life gets for you, your health, your family, and your world—IT'S UP TO YOU TO NEVER GIVE UP! Life can be unpleasant more times than not, but there are a few lessons I have learned firsthand. My favorite echo is from my great grandmother:

Life never takes you where you want to go. It only takes you where you need to go.

Wants and needs are always fighting for the spotlight in our lives. When she told me this, and repeated it often, I didn't understand the weight of her words. She was a preacher for an old church at the end of the old orange clay road in the middle of orange groves. Full of light and hope, she was a blessing in my life, and I am thankful for the time I was able to spend with her.

She was right.

My life has given me some unexpected terrifying moments. Once the dust settled, I was calm enough to reflect on the events; I realized there was hidden need for those moments to push me down a path more fitting to bring happier times. I didn't plan to be an author, but when I became a cancer survivor, a new mom, holding a foreclosure notice to my dream home and on the verge of a layoff, it forced me to take my writing career seriously. This was a life changer—the soul food I didn't know I needed. Moving forward, I developed my own mantra:

Don't be my own obstacle.

It was a promise to me. Life throws some curveballs, things we can't control, and all we can do at times is simply wait out the storm and pick up the pieces afterwards. That's okay. It happens. What you can do is make a promise to yourself. Remember not to self-sabotage or let yourself mourn or stay stagnant for too long. If you want something, and the only thing stopping you is hesitation, then act. Break your own mold, find a way to break free of self-doubt in small ways, and eventually, you'll find the only obstacles left are the ones you can't control.

Thirteen Years of Tribulations

Life is unpredictable. Despite some wild high and low moments, I'm still writing, publishing, and sharing what I learn every chance I have. You may or may not know me. No, I'm not a best-selling author (yet). Yes, I'm an award-winning author when I enter into the contests that exist out there, but the question really is: what qualifies me of all the authors in the sea, worthy of writing a book such as this? If I had the money and a calmer chain of events in my life, I would be a best-selling writer. Let's be ambitious and honest. There's nothing more inspiring than seeing the light in another writer's eyes as you help them overcome writer's block or provide some tools they didn't realize they had in their arsenal.

Whether you want to call it "paying it forward" or "giving back to the writing community," it comes down to one fact: I love to share what I discover about writing and publishing. I'm also not one to rush into anything without research or, at best, experimenting to see things firsthand. There's a ton of advice out there, and sometimes I can't help but wonder if what echoes down that narrow hallway is truly beneficial for the all or for the one. This book is one way I get to share what I've learned, experienced, and even shared from all manner of people in the publishing and writing industries.

Ah, but who am I? What do I write? Where did I come from?

I'm a sixth-generation Floridian (on the same road!) who, through a series of unfortunate events, discovered her calling to write and create books. It wasn't obvious or a straight and narrow answer. In fact, the amount of tribulation I have faced in my life, and even now as I begin *The Writer's Bane*, makes me painfully aware that I have a fortitude like no other. Or simply put, I'm too stubborn to quit.

My heart is a lush for mixed genres that carry a lot of the values from genres like paranormal romance, dark fantasy, dark romance, epic fantasy, mythology, historical fiction, and even memoir. Like many of my fellow writers, I did a lot of writing and doodling in my younger years. The most profound was a filled composition book in fifth grade. Though my mother didn't approve and pushed for me to be a doctor or a lawyer, I never stopped. Not everyone has the endurance to watch their journals and creations tossed in a trashcan while they are ordered to stop writing—and still keep going. If only I knew being an historian was a legitimate occupation, the world might have missed out on this bookworm completely.

One of my favorite genres to read growing up was fantasy, more specifically, fantasy that is dark in tone and filled with paranormal and mythology elements. Add in a sprinkle of historical references and I am SOLD. It has always amazed me how authors create such wonderful worlds and stories with such depth. I'm glad to share my own worlds and characters with readers in hopes of inspiring future writers. At times, I feel like I'm giving back what those authors gave to me: an adventure and escape when life seemed dreadful, a lesson I didn't know I needed told through a life not my own.

My early reads circled between three authors: C.S. Lewis, R.L. Stine, and Lewis Carroll. Later, this evolved to include Robin McKinley, Cat Adams, James Clavell, Anne Rice, and Neil Gaiman. Before I stumbled on these wonderful authors, I had only read non-fiction books about drawing or animals (outside of the mandatory readings assigned by my elementary school teachers). Needless to say, I read every Zoo Book the library had, sometimes twice. From there, like many of my generation,

I dove into R.L. Stine's famous Goosebumps series, but I have never enjoyed horror books beyond this scope. That doesn't mean I didn't read the genre, trying out Stephen King, Michael Crichton, and others. I even found there was a specific type of horror that leaned into the dark fantasy realm. And yet, I still continued the search for *my* genre.

It didn't take long to find C. S. Lewis and Lewis Carroll who showed me fantastical worlds that were just beyond the wardrobe or rabbit hole. These were wonderful, delightful reads, but something was still missing. Soon, I discovered another genre through James Clavell, historical fiction, where I realized that amazing fictional stories could stay true to the events and settings around them. This discovery spiraled into a search for something that blended the two genres. It was like a scavenger hunt, and I aimed to satisfy all my wants in a good book.

Discovering Elizabeth Kostova's *The Historian* opened up the door and added something new. The enjoyment I received from reading a paranormal story heavily involving the history of Vlad the Impaler was off the scales. This idea, this dark flavor that smeared the lines of fantasy, horror, and history was the flavor I had been searching for and aspired to write. It was okay to show the dark workings of characters. They didn't have to be perfect. It was the flaws in Edmund and the characters in the previous books that made them feel so real, even when devoured by dinosaurs or described as talking beavers.

Through my interactions with these wonderful authors and their stories, I started to decide what I wanted my own readers to experience. This concept seemed to help build a foundation for my storytelling early on, looking to my own favorite books for insight on what experience did I take from that and how I could mimic that in my own way within my own stories. Some of the key elements were flawed characters, writing to cater all audiences, showing love is more than the act or the kiss, and the raw moments people exchange when no one is watching. I wanted all these in my stories!

Tattooed Angels Trilogy has been a labor of love project. It's responsible for my drive to become an author and the desire to share my work with others. There are profound moments in a writer's life, and this trilogy had a large part in my own. Throughout elementary and middle school, I was a tenacious reader with a love for fantasy books. I wrote my first novel in fifth grade. I still have the composition book I filled front to back, covered in assorted stickers from the 1990's (with the map I drew glued into the back cover).

One fateful night during my high school days, Tattooed Angels was born. I recall the clock pushing past midnight as I tried to lull myself to sleep listening to some rock music. The DJ came on, talking about this new release from a band called TOOL. In the black abyss of night, I took in the heartbeat intro of the song *Laterlus*. The first few lyrics played out, the idea of black and white, then colors started a chain reaction in my imagination. It was here, lost to the music, I started asking myself a series of questions.

> *What kind of character would be like that? Someone who normally sees in black and white, but on occasion might see something in color... Oh! What if he was color blind, but it was actually secret powers he gained from reincarnation? Wait... I got it. What if he's a failed reincarnation? Hmm, what kind of powers would...*

It went on and on and before I knew it, I was jotting the brainstorm down, doodling some sketches, and the morning alarm was blasting. It all started with the creation of Hotan, then asking what kind of character he was, what his story was, and what I wanted him to share with readers.

During high school, I faced a lot of complicated situations. My parents were getting divorced, my father was lost to alcoholism (He's now sober, and we've made amends), my mother's verbal abuse started becoming physical (we don't talk and attempts for counseling have failed), and I felt broken. While my friends fretted over boyfriends, parties, and popularity, I felt all alone in my own goals. I needed a job, I kept good grades, and I aimed for independence as soon as possible.

I needed a dependable place to call home or at least a place where I could feel safe.

In a lot of ways, Hotan reflected me. An adult in a teen's body, I earned the name "mother hen" because I took care of my friends, keeping them out of trouble or helping them with their schoolwork. Because everything at home was so unstable behind closed doors, I focused on being my own pillar and a cornerstone for my friends. I didn't discuss what was happening, though many of my teachers had an inkling. It was probably hard to miss the quiet kid coming early to school and crying in a dark corner.

Anyhow, Hotan was my vehicle to deliver a message to my friends and other teens while letting others learn from my mistakes. The name Hotan was originally inspired by a Japanese language website claiming it meant "origin, starting point," but that isn't accurate at all. In fact, it's more fitting to acknowledge Hotan is Biblical Greek for "when, inasmuch," which is ironic and fits even more.

Aiming to deliver a message, I started a cautionary tale, one which encouraged asking for help, especially for the hard stuff, and refusing to hide. My story showed how to speak up, accepted the idea that life is unpredictable, and reassured readers that even though it may feel as if the world is against them, the fight is normal. Life is a struggle—and that's okay.

By the time high school ended, I had twenty-five thousand hard-earned words. Many times, I lost my creation and had to start over. One time, the computer died; another time, the floppy disk was destroyed. Still worse was the time my mother trashed my work, ripping it up, and even setting a sketchbook on fire. I didn't give up. I started hiding parts of the story in the back of my math and animal science notebooks. I even printed the current copy out, put it in a binder, and asked a friend to keep it at her house. This was one thing no one could take from me: my desire to tell a story.

Life became a wild rollercoaster after I graduated. I was working several jobs and launched into college full time. The story collected dust in a box I carried, but I was hellbent on never going back home. I even lived out of my truck for a while. Years passed, and the story was forgotten until I ran into some friends I hadn't seen since high school.

"Did you ever finish that story about Hotan?"

The question rattled me. I had forgotten about the story, but somehow, it had made an impression on them. They wanted to know if it was done, if there was an end to Hotan's tale. So, I blew off the dust, figured out where I left off, and finished the story. With no fear of someone destroying it, I finished the story in a little over fifty-thousand words.

I gave it to a few friends to read and enjoy, but life hit me again, and the story found itself shelved. At least I had managed to pull together how book two and three would flow. Ah, but a book can't write itself! I went to school for Graphic Design (I was part of the ITT debacle and was one class shy of my degree), then Game Programming, but health issues interfered, and I resigned.

Things settled for a little while, but I found myself in the most insane six months of my life. The economy popped. Our new house of barely two years, bought with equity, was now far below. The construction industry left me and my husband laid off. On top of that, I fell horribly ill, unable to keep water or food down, so the mother-in-law took me to the hospital.

"Good news! You're about a month along in your pregnancy!"

I paled. We had been trying for three years, but we had only lost our jobs two weeks before. Of course, this would stick at the worst moment ever. Within the same month, a freckle on the back of my left calf became a monstrous mole. I cried and pleaded with the doctors to biopsy. My great grandmother had one in the same spot. I knew what it meant by the look and the speed with which it grew. It took another month before a doctor heard me out.

"I'm so sorry. You were right. This is an atypical melanoma, and we need to remove it immediately."

Here I was staring at the results while pushing into four months pregnant with my first child. I couldn't believe how hard my life fell apart: twenty-four hour "morning" sickness, both of us laid off through 2009-2010 winter, mortgage company speeding up our foreclosure because we let them know "no job and stage three cancer diagnosis." I cried. Then I cried some more. Doctors called and told me where to be, sometimes the night before for a morning appointment. So many tears were shed. It all seemed unfair. This was too much—just one of these events would be enough to break a person.

In the end, they removed the back of my left calf while I was awake, a scary experience since I'd never even had a stitch or broken a bone before. I managed to shut down the foreclosure, very aware of the medical clause in my contract, sending them the football stitching down my leg and the intimate reports from the surgery with "stage 3"

and "pregnant" highlighted. It was hell recovering, puking, and moving.

I sat there as our new hovel rattled. The house we thought we would never leave sold in a quick sale. Recovering with a newborn, I was alone while my husband landed a job working long hours for half the pay. Looking around, I saw my books, the boxes I could never let go—that had lived in a truck with me—these were part of my soul.

"Maybe I should do something with that novel from high school... leave something behind for our kid."

That one thought drove me to learn how to write at a professional level and publish my work. I had a memorable story, but I needed to know what it would take to make it an actual book. The answer left me crying once more: to fix it, to bring it to industry standard, required one more rewrite. A flood of sour memories followed, but this was the best decision ever.

"It's part of life to struggle. Just makes those good days that much sweeter..."

And thus, my career as an author and the start of Tattooed Angels Trilogy was born!

With these tools and inspiration, my desire for writing was renewed. I still needed helping hands from family and friends to make sure I didn't give up on my writing goals, but I finally made it. My next story, *Cedric: The Demonic Knight*, took its background from both history books and long forgotten lore and bestiaries. It took some heavy searching to dig out information on all things werewolf, vampire, and more importantly, mythology. My single wish was to expose my readers to intriguing concepts, opening the door to a time period and lore that has been skewed from the original telling. I want my readers to experience the lore firsthand, and when the conversation came up in class or at the café among friends, they had the facts etched into their hearts. I wanted to hear them say,

THIRTEEN YEARS OF TRIBULATIONS

school (circa 2001-2003). When I started writing this piece, I wanted it to be able to go into my high school's library and share some hard lessons about selfhood and those harder moments in our lives. I made it to Chapter Six before life swept me away from it. It collected dust until it somehow came up in a conversation at work in 2005. At that time, a friend named Kelly inspired and encouraged me to continue writing. The next year, I added to it, pushing to Chapter 12 before I let life wipe it from my thoughts again.

In 2010, I found myself part of an online gaming group called *The Shadow Legion*. Somehow someone (Ruth and Ruth, along with Susannah) reminded me I had *Rebirth* waiting on me to complete. Thanks to the encouragements of my Gaming Crew, I finished my first rough draft of a complete novel. Looking back, I had no idea how significant it was for any writer to finish the story. Unfortunately, that wasn't the end of my frustration. I realized as I researched more about the professional writing field that *Rebirth* needed a mountain of work—a rewrite of my high school portions. I can't tell you how many times I sat in front of my computer staring at a screen of text, no idea how to even begin a rewrite or how to break myself away from the original writing to make a better version.

At this point, I entertained the idea of sketching out a graphic novel. There were obstacles to that piece as well. I found myself throwing out storyboard after storyboard on how to capture everything I wanted to tell the audience in this epic idea. Looking at both of these stories, *Rebirth* and *Cedric*, I had to make some hard decisions.

Rebirth deserved quality writing and attention...

...but I wasn't skilled enough, not yet. *Cedric*, on the other hand, still wasn't giving enough for the reader to see. I knew I would come to points that needed large paragraphs to explain. It hit me: take what I now knew about writing and write *Cedric* instead.

At this point, *Cedric* had three years of random research, sketches, and roughed out storyline plots. It took a year to get the whole story down in the rough and another year to refine, but *Cedric* finally made it to print, and I gained a mountain of experience in this new world where I'm called author.

"I know it because I lived it through Cedric/Romasanta/Lillith," and smile.

Currently, I have completed my young adult dark urban fantasy trilogy, Tattooed Angels. The first book in this series is *Rebirth*, a story I put to paper back in high

Am I ready to fix Rebirth?

Holding my breath, I opened that old Word .doc file and loaded the other half of the screen with a fresh .doc file. I started to rewrite the story with tears streaming down my face. Glancing over the first chapter, I grimaced, seeing the mistakes; I could see where I didn't think of my readers' needs. There were clear moments where my fear of revealing too much derailed the content. I have since learned that if it's a good story and beautifully written, I can tell readers everything and still pull them in. That first night I pumped out over 5,000 words, expanding the first chapter so much it had to be split in two!

Progress had been made.

A full-time author was born. I haven't stopped or looked back since, and I hope to write many more stories, novels, and series. If life didn't seem wild so far, 2018 tested me on so many levels. Once more, the tribulations stacked up: my dad's double lung transplant, my mother-in-law's broken arm, me father-in-law's knee surgery and kidney problems, my littlest one's autism and need for tubes, my diagnosis of Alpha-1 (which killed dad's lungs), and so much more.

I felt drained.

Despite it all, I wrote the final book of the Tattooed Angels Trilogy, finished another book concept to query to agents, remade a few public domain reference books, hosted workshops and webinars, and spoke on panels as a guest author for MegaCon Tampa Bay & Orlando. Part of the reason for my success is that I both gave and accepted help from many others in the community. This included the Alliance of Worldbuilders founded on Authonomy before it fell, and later, in my local area, Writer's Atelier and its founder Racquel Henry. Without their guidance and encouragement, I wouldn't be writing this book or any of the books I have published, completed, and brainstormed.

I had my moments of self-doubt, even after being gushed over for the work I had achieved after only a book or two. No, self-publishing wasn't my initial aim. I wanted to be traditional, but some amazing literary agents gave me some great advice about my work and what it would take to make it into a book and get it into reader's hands. In the end, I don't fit in a box. My work is often hard to market since I don't cater a hundred percent to fantasy or romance... or paranormal or historical or mythology. My books are a mixed bag, but in a good way.

Never stop moving forward.

I never stopped. As my mantra implies, I am in control of my writing and what happens to it. Today, I find myself with contracts, sitting at tables at my favorite conventions and inspiring writers every chance I have. Keep going. It will be hard and ugly, but I promise, there's light at the end of this, and that curse will become a blessing.

"We got this! Let's go write a story!"

TABLE OF CONTENTS

The Research

Research is to see what everybody else has seen,
and to think what nobody else has thought.
ALBERT SZENT-GYORGYI

INTRODUCTION

First, you should know you don't need to do research in order to write a story. There's no wrong or right way to carry out your research either. This section is designed to give writers an idea of different ways to use research and strategies for staying focused on the important things. A story has several pieces, like characters, world, and plot; your research should reflect these different elements. The imagination can lead to some strange places while we create amazing individuals who live out their lives on the pages of books, but beware!

Real life can often be stranger than fiction.

In the scope of my own research, I used real life to my advantage while weaving amazing tales for my readers. As writers, we often need research, and some stories need more than others. Naturally curious creatures, we are driven to satisfy our thirst to see where *this* goes. In many of our stories, characters and worlds have elements we have never experienced (or want to), things new to our lives that we need to learn more about before we can effectively write about them. And while not all research feels fun, it can be easy to fall down a rabbit-hole, coming up for air hours later to realize we've been diving into unnecessary information (for the current project). The internet may be a great way to procrastinate, but it is still one of the most useful research tools of the 21st Century.

This section contains my breakdown, advice, and techniques involving research. Take what applies to you and your genre and leave the rest, but I aim to inspire. This section is great to help break writer's block, aid in plotting,

enhance character development, detail world building, and even ease revisions.

For the sake of clarity, I will be pulling a personal example from my novel, *Romasanta: Father of Werewolves*, along with some of my favorite movies, books, and television shows for comparison.

Alert: Spoilers ahead!

However, these references are the best way to connect research with a final piece. If you have attended any of my webinars or workshops, you'll know I use popular movies and shows to make that connection more quickly, despite a mixed bag of writers in the audience. There's something here for everyone.

WARNING: WATCH OUT FOR RABBIT-HOLES!

You read that right: you can find yourself falling down the rabbit-hole much like Alice when it comes to research. It's easy to get excited, seeing some new piece of information that tickles your fancy and within a matter of minutes, you're gone. Hours later, you've spent more time chasing snippets for several stories rather than doing research for the current one.

To help you stay on task, I want to share what I do to stay focused. Though it's more along the lines of a pep talk or even an emergency evacuation for when you venture near a rabbit-hole, these items also double as great aids for brainstorming and creating outlines. This part even includes some worksheets you can use to stay on point. Think of it as my way of keeping the *Titanic* from hitting that iceberg.

DECIDE ON A FOCUS

Break your research into smaller parts. A hyper-focused goal is easier to control. The first step is deciding if you want to focus on a character, your world, or the plot. This technique will help any writer, whether character-driven like me, world-driven like Tolkien, or plot-driven like George R.R. Martin. Decide on one aspect. If you plan to focus on a character, you may need to flesh out what they do for a living, be it warrior, blacksmith, or watchmaker. Worldbuilding can be broken down to environment, culture, or even history. As for plot, this usually is situational more than anything else. It pulls a little from both world and character but requires more. For example, an earthquake is happening in the story to force your characters to... end up together? Separated? Injured?

- Decide on a Focus for:
  - Character (Ex. "Blacksmiths" or "Archery")
  - World (Ex. "Cold Climates" or "Persian Empire Culture")
  - Plot Points (Ex. "Great Chicago Fires" or "Bonnie & Clyde Capture")

- Character: Romasanta
  - Apollo
  - Werewolf
  - Tie in Emanuel Romasanta

MAKE A WANT LIST

Think of it as creating a playlist made up of your research goodies. Granted, this needs to mesh with your current focus. Each character, town, and plot point in your story will have its own research candy. You can set overlapping wants. For example, when it came to research for The Cedric Series, I aimed for mythology, legends, lore, and history older than the 13th and 12th centuries. That didn't mean I wouldn't break this rule when I saw a related opening, but it helped lay a foundation of consistency. When I started on book two, *Romasanta*, my Want List shifted to focus on werewolf lore that spanned all of history in order to bring readers up to speed. As I came across each new want, I wrote it down and took a step forward.

✒ My Want List for *Romasanta: Father of Werewolves*

- 🐾 Lycan and Werewolf lore
- 🐾 Predating 12th Century
- 🐾 Medieval lore
- 🐾 Tie in Emanuel Romasanta from 1800's
- 🐾 Apollo lore
- 🐾 Lean towards Romanian lore as base for werewolf curse

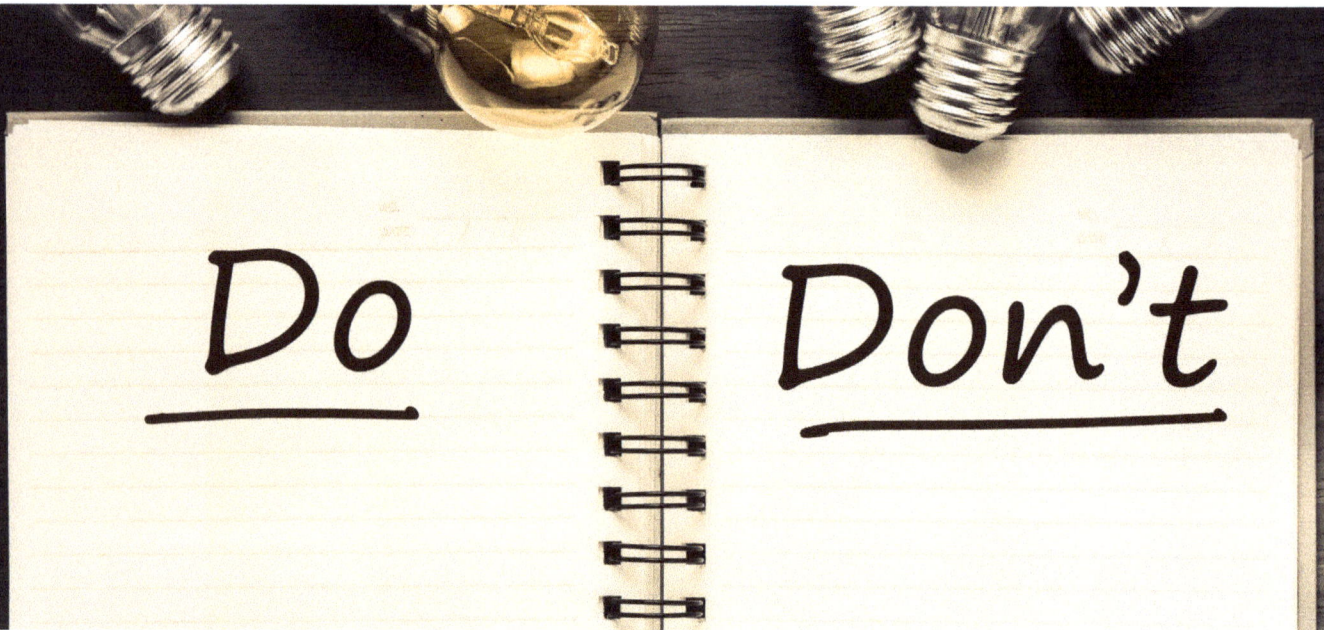

MAKE A DON'T LIST

Can't think of what you want? You're not alone! When I needed a song list for my wedding, I blanked, but then they asked for a "don't play" list instead! What an amazing concept! Sometimes it's easier to say what you don't want. This is also a great question to keep you from falling into any rabbit-holes. Listing the negatives is a great way to discover your desires for a character. It will also help you make those hard decisions. The moment your research doesn't feel right, add it to the Don't List. When this happens, add to your Want List instead! You might be surprised how this simple task can help you focus.

✒ My Don't List for *Romasanta: Father of Werewolves*

- 🐾 No guns or gunpowder
- 🐾 Nothing newer than 12th century myths
- 🐾 Not Apollo the Sun God (Yes, there is more than one Apollo!)
- 🐾 Nothing that falls into pop culture werewolf lore

DECLARE YOUR TOPIC

Put it on a sticky note, write it down, and say it aloud. I don't know precisely why, but completing ANY GOAL without taking this step seems harder. Simply thinking about your topic makes it a secret easily forgotten. STOP! Shout your topic from the rooftops, tell someone else about it, and schedule time for research ("research hour at 2 pm for *Romasanta*"). This psychological trigger may surprise you. Build accountability with yourself and defend the time you devote your writing. Don't make this less important than the rest of your life, or you'll have a hard time finishing your book.

✐ Declaration for *Romasanta: Father of Werewolves*

- ✎ "Main character, who is a merchant in the Dark Ages, combined with wolf lore and legends pre-dating 12th century who isn't the same as the Pop Culture werewolf versions I see on XYZ show"
- ✎ Declaration for *Judgment* from Tattooed Angel Trilogy
- ✎ "World disasters, from 1700 and older, complete towns or areas wiped out, pivotal trade towns"

✐ Other Examples from Mainstream Media

- ✎ "Ice Climate, dangerous, large predators who can live in permafrost areas. No human or off-world beings can survive a storm without shelter or dire measures." [The planet Hoth from *Star Wars*]
- ✎ "Bring a prehistoric disease back to life, set it loose, and make it give birth to vampires like those seen in history like Vlad. Main character contracts disease but doesn't turn. His friend turns, and no matter what, they can't join forces. Oh, and main character sucks at relationships." [*V Wars* by Jonathan Mayberry]
- ✎ "Two hobbits must survive the most treacherous quest to destroy a cursed ring. They can't use the ring (anyone who holds or touches ring goes mad), and everyone wants it and will kill to have it. Ring makes you invisible but summons crazy scary creatures to hunt you down." [*Lord of the Rings* by Tolkien]

BUT I FOUND THIS THING FOR MY OTHER STORY...

No! Put it down! Look away! Actually, if it's that good, copy the link (or title and page number), write a quick note, and keep it for another day. Research for one story often leads to gold nuggets for another, but you need to stay focused. You don't want to derail future projects, but you can't lose your momentum on the current topic. This would be a good time to add this tidbit to the "Don't" list for the current focus and the "Want" list for another.

Your other "Want" list should be the carrot on a string for your self-motivation. You can't research that cool thing until you finish the current focus. Sometimes, I forget these nuggets, so when I open up the research file or notebook for the next project, I am excited all over again. I get to chase these caves and veins now, things I had forgotten about. In fact, a great time to circle back is after completing the first draft of a story. Take a step back, break out, and reward yourself. For a research hound like me, this break helps me disconnect and thereby improve revision and editing in the story I just finished—while prepping the next project. Double win!

STOP OFTEN & REVIEW YOUR NOTES

Don't forget the value of taking a break. For sanity's sake, never try to do all your research for a book in one chunk. It's perfectly fine to start drafting a story and dive into research as the need arises. I have witnessed authors derail a first draft by thinking they had to get everything plotted and researched in advance. Granted, everyone is different, and I have seen authors use this method and succeed, but it's not for me. The bottom line is that you need to find your happy median between research and drafting. Some of you may prefer to write the story and research as you do your revisions to strengthen weak parts. Regardless, review your notes often. Make sure that you understand what is happening and why. When you compare your focus, "Don't" list, "Want" list, and overall story idea, they should all lineup.

Taking a break is also a great way to come up for air and see where you need to aim next. Set a timer to stop digging and look over what you've found. This is usually when I find I skipped something and can refocus on a new branch of research I almost missed out on. Breaks can also keep you from burning out on one idea and allow you to pull in other concepts. This is also time to question your focus and decide if it needs to shift. YES, you can change the initial parameters of the research now that you've learned more about the topic. I promise it's okay! This is also a good time to ask if you have enough research to start writing or if you should switch focus to another character, worldbuilding, or plot point.

IN CONCLUSION...

Don't let research be the enabler of procrastination. There is no reason why you can't start writing first and lean back on research when you get stuck. I've had to do this a few times and often suggest things or share videos on items I think can shed some light on a story. There are plenty of moments when a reader comes across a character or story element that doesn't quite feel right. Research can aid with this, whether looking online, emailing someone, or even visiting a place for personal insight. That small gesture goes a long way in how we portray different elements within our writing, affecting how readers (who may or may not know about that topic) perceive our stories.

- Largest Lepers colony in Medieval times
- Largest trading hub in Medieval times
- Who are the Keretes?

✎ Examples of Researched Topics I've suggested or done

- Make soap from Animal Fat
- How to check the health of a horse
- Walking behind waterfalls
- How to make horseshoes
- Skinning a rabbit
- Different levels of burns
- Does skin melt?
- What plants were found in Biblical times?
- What was the weather like in Biblical times?
- Branding
- Buzz Buttons are used for...?
- When was Vodka made?

ACTIVITY: DECLARE YOUR FOCUS

		Want	**Don't**
Characters	Main Character Romasanta	Emanuel Romasanta history; Apollo; Oracle tie-in; Wolves; Older shapeshifter lore; Ancient Greek foundation	Pop Culture; None of that sparkly vampire versions; Insta-control of shift; I don't want the curse aspect permanent
	Character Fenrir	To play of the Nordic lores but also cross into Shinto Forest God and Greek mythology; This should be the essence of all werewolves through his need for a pack	Make him too human; Always circling back to being simply a dog/wolf;
	Character Nyctimus	Bring out more of the forgotten history and lore around the Lykaon;	Stay away from legend involving Zeus and Pan; Not a competition to gain Daphne/Pitip's love
Worldbuilding	Home The Farm	At peaces, humbling; No ambitions besides simply living; willing to protect this life at all costs.	Nothing bad happens to home. Too cliche. Double down on Lykaon history here.
	Place The Forest	Black Forest, ancient, top predator, eats everything and destructive; Always at his wildest here	Not necessarily always freeing; no lingering humanity in most cases
	Place The Streets	Forgotten; an abandonment of the wild or possibly a fear of returning to the bloodlust	Rich, leading a pack, new love but old love ok. I don't want these things by the end of the story and have his living condition show it.
Plot Points	Main Plot Find the Stone	A constant reach for it with clues and close calls. Cedric is the key	Not easy to find, had it and lost it. This should be an impossible task.
	Obstacle The Curse	Share his body. Should be a sense of Rom becoming more wolf and Fen becoming more human until he leaves.	No lost of wolf, amp up wolfiness. Not easy to hide.
	Obstacle "You're only a man"	A reminder of his flaws and mistakes; A reminder he is trying to get his wife back.	I don't want him to go with the flow. He's a softy and will agonize over EVERYTHING.

ACTIVITY: DECLARE YOUR FOCUS

		Want	Don't
Characters	Main Character		
	Character		
	Character		
Worldbuilding	Home		
	Place		
	Place		
Plot Points	Main Plot		
	Obstacle		
	Obstacle		

ACTIVITY: DECLARE YOUR FOCUS

		Want	Don't
Characters	Main Character		
	Character		
	Character		
Worldbuilding	Home		
	Place		
	Place		
Plot Points	Main Plot		
	Obstacle		
	Obstacle		

ACTIVITY: DECLARE YOUR FOCUS

		Want	Don't
Characters	Main Character		
	Character		
	Character		
Worldbuilding	Home		
	Place		
	Place		
Plot Points	Main Plot		
	Obstacle		
	Obstacle		

ACTIVITY: DECLARE YOUR FOCUS

		Want	Don't
Characters	Main Character		
	Character		
	Character		
Worldbuilding	Home		
	Place		
	Place		
Plot Points	Main Plot		
	Obstacle		
	Obstacle		

ACTIVITY: DECLARE YOUR FOCUS

		Want	Don't
Characters	Main Character		
	Character		
	Character		
Worldbuilding	Home		
	Place		
	Place		
Plot Points	Main Plot		
	Obstacle		
	Obstacle		

TYPES OF RESEARCH

When I say types, I'm not talking about the different genres (romance, horror, memoir, and so on), nor am I implying the different research sources at this stage. In fact, most authors rely on the internet most of all due to its speed, access, and privacy. We make jokes or see memes often about odd search histories, but it's true. Some of my personal Google.com searches include:

Making soap with
animal fat
Top male fetishes
Are necropants real?
Were all the alchemists
named Hermes?

The internet search bar offers no boundaries to the bizarre questions developing in a writer's mind during research. Whether you aim for historical accuracy or to spark your imagination, articles, images, and videos await your discovery. Don't limit yourself to just the internet for resources—venture out! If you plan on writing about a historical fishing or mining town, make a day trip to one. The stories and visuals from the town historian are gold (rarely something you can find on the internet). Plus, you can make someone's day by asking questions and showing interest in their hometown's back story.

You have a focus.

Right now, you've managed to focus on a character, world, or events for the plot. Depending on your genre, some of these will be heavier than others. Each story can have different demands in these three sections. Below, I have broken the research into three core sections:

WORLD
CHARACTER
PLOT POINTS

I will walk you through these in this order since this is how I begin the process of outlining my own story ideas. Make sure you have your tools and anti-rabbit-hole lists ready and by your side. Even better, set a timer to remind yourself to come up for air and re-evaluate where you are and where you need to go in your efforts.

I break each research scope into subcategories in an effort to capture a wide variety of angles. I don't always find the answer to every section, but the quest slows me down to ask vital questions—which often lead to deeper writing, even for a character-driven piece. These details should provide enough input for the senses and immerse the readers (and characters) in unique ways.

VALERIE WILLIS

WORLDBUILDING RESEARCH

I f you're writing historical fiction or setting your story in a different time or place, this section will help with one of the more important aspects of your story. Worldbuilding reflects the time period, setting, place, ambience, and even mechanics or laws of the world your characters live in. Research for this can vary depending on your needs and wants.

Contemporary, romance, and urban fantasy writers may find this section unnecessary or on the light side. I do recommend glancing over it, especially the world mechanics. Not every "Modern Times" piece can skip this section. In my own writing in this genre, I still dive onto Google Maps and similar sites to discover local hotels, attractions, and even a café or local store to see what the streets look like there.

Is it busy?
Are there more cars
than bikes?
Or more pedestrians
than vehicles?

When immersing readers into your story, the world plays a large role in the process. You must make them believe you stood there in Cairo. Let them feel the environment like the characters in your story. Whether you're in Cairo, Georgia during a balmy, mosquito-laden summer or in the middle of a sandstorm in Cairo, Egypt will be up to how well you incorporate the research into your description.

For example, I read this excerpt from my book *The Oracle* at an Open Mic event:

> The sky was a brilliant gold with brush strokes of dark peach floating above the purple mountain range. Angeline gripped the wooden rail of the wrought iron balcony, taking it all in. They had been there for a few hours, but the view from their room at the *Fedriades Delphi Hotel* still stunned her. Flying here had been thrilling and frightening. There were so many new things for her to discover, all made by human hands. Her heart raced, taking in this new and exotic place called *Greece*. The beauty of the landscape was romantic with the setting sun deepening to match the terracotta tiles of the buildings. Behind her, Cedric entered through the door. Their eyes met, and her face flushed. Since the Busse, those sharp green eyes had softened their edge, and it frightened her.
>
> His eyes fell away from her, guilt crossing his face. "usleave at midnight for the *Temple of Athena Pronoia*."
>
> Turning away, she swallowed her thoughts back down. "I-it's so beautiful here."
>
> Cedric wrapped his arms around her tight, pulling her into him. "Then I'll bring you back here after this is done..."

Afterward, one of the audience members sought me out to ask, "You lived in Delphi? So did I!"

This reaction was definitely a compliment of my writing skills—to impress someone who had seen the hotel in person, walked the streets, and even understood the later reference of the lights and guards at the temple. I aim for this reaction any time I recreate a place: real, forgotten, or fantasy. I want my readers to chase my story through the forest and cities on foot!

GEOGRAPHICAL

What place, city, region, environment, location, or landmarks are you aiming to recreate or even construct? Think of the physical aspects of the habitat, planet, or location. How do these details affect your story? How can they allow for certain plot events or build skills and knowledge within your characters?

Look at your own experience in relation to where you've lived and how that influenced your skill and knowledge set. Raised in Florida all my life, I personally know a lot about the southern environment, wildlife, tourism, hidden local getaways, fishing, and even Disney World—just because of where I live. This background gives me knowledge in areas non-Floridians might not think about.

Placing a water goddess on a desert planet in a science fiction story would have a different effect than a water goddess in a waterfall temple within the rainforest. Instantly, the environment influences the weight of the story here. It's safe to assume the desert would pray for rain or water, while the rainforest might worship a being who reigns supreme in this element, assuming this is her territory since it's waterlogged.

In richer fantasy stories, the story takes advantage of this. Whether it's Star Wars, Tolkien, or George R.R. Martin, each uses changing environments and cultures to push and pull the story. Tatooine and its sand people differs drastically from Hoth and its Tauntauns (a snow lizard of sorts). The abandoned dwarven city of Khazad-dum hints at a very different culture and architecture than the elven city Lothlorien. And let's not forget how different even the Stark's homebase Winterfell seemed compared to King's Landing. Even the city names hint at the expected purpose and atmosphere.

Despite all the seeming differences, these stories all required similar research. Cold environments, permafrost tribes, clothing for extreme cold; which fur does best in a cold environment; what animals live there; signs of hyperthermia; signs of frost bite; can fuel freeze; how fast does water freeze at negative thirty? Often the best method of research is to ask questions and find the answer. In the process, you find answers you didn't know you needed to write a convincing scene. All three of these creators drastically diverged in how they incorporated the cold environment into their worlds and stories.

You may see or hear the terms "progressive" and "traditional" thrown out there in the industry and within the pages of this book. Keep in mind that a progressive location, society, or culture is in a constant state of change. They are making progress, for better or worse, with technology and constantly changing how they are evolving. For example, the Death Star in *Star Wars* would be an example of a progressive location. It's completely manmade and the latest and greatest in planetary destruction.

Traditional locations, cultures, and so forth tend to have a satisfactory means of living. They hold on to a traditional way of handling things, rarely changing how they go about things. In comparison, this would be our most beloved Mandalorians in *Star Wars*. Granted, a traditional location in the real world would be like the tribes of the Amazon forest, small towns that still do things like the founding fathers, and so forth. Being able to decide which is more fitting can make strong contrasting locations within a single story and world. "This is the way."

Another way to see this contrast is to ask: if this is a cold planet, are they using progressive hi-tech to stay warm or more traditional means like Eskimo on dog sleds? Even then, don't underestimate the means of combining a little of both. Since we're on a *Star Wars* kick, a great one for this is the Planet Hoth and the base there. Yes, they are using tech, but readers still see them running around using the local fauna to their advantage, riding on Tauntauns. And while we're considering the terrain, it's time to think more specifically about geography.

What kind of fauna and flora exist in your setting, if any at all? I love watching documentaries on extreme environments or places that remind me of what I am writing. It's amazing to see how different the seasons and storms can be, especially learning how the life there handles everything.

When it comes to fauna, the wildlife, decide how aggressive they are and how they would react to the invasion of your characters. If this was the world of *Jumanji*, then everything wants to eat or destroy you, even the animals normally considered docile refuse to run away. Look at the ratio of predator versus prey for guidance. Even then, the way they interact with the characters can depend on where they fall on the food pyramid. Prey can be deadly, like in *Avatar*, or the planet can be like the *Care Bears* where nothing is harmful.

The same applies to flora, the plant life in a place. Often in science fiction, readers see characters facing plants that move like fauna, eating and snatching things up at will. Other times, like Alice, they have conversations with poppy flowers the size of a small hut. Fantasy realms usually have a miracle healing plant or magic booster of sorts when processed and consumed. The environments can shift with jungle plants to a desert-scape where only tumbleweeds and cacti grow. Defining the kind of fauna can shift how anyone sees your world.

ACTIVITY: DEFINING GEOGRAPHY

Name	Location	Weather

Progressive Traditional Combo	Fauna	Flora

ACTIVITY: DEFINING GEOGRAPHY

Name	Location	Weather

Progressive Traditional Combo	Fauna	Flora

ACTIVITY: DEFINING GEOGRAPHY

Name	Location	Weather

Progressive Traditional Combo	Fauna	Flora

ACTIVITY: DEFINING GEOGRAPHY

Name	Location	Weather

Progressive Traditional Combo	Fauna	Flora

ACTIVITY: DEFINING GEOGRAPHY

Name	Location	Weather

Progressive Traditional Combo	Fauna	Flora

ACTIVITY: DEFINING GEOGRAPHY

Name	Location	Weather

Progressive Traditional Combo	Fauna	Flora

TIMELINE OR TIME PERIOD

Whether you are writing time travel, historical, or steampunk, you need to know about the time period you use. The time period limits what is available or even achievable by your characters. Often, magic or another plot device can overcome limitations based on these restrictions. Perhaps aliens have landed and mingled with the humans, leaving pyramids all over the world and advancing the technology tenfold!

Historical fiction often romanticizes a way of living from a certain decade or century. Some in this genre aim to capture historical events using fictional characters. Others focus on a creative retelling of a real person's life, whether Benjamin Franklin or Joan of Arc. The latter tends to be popular in video media, including the video game *Assassin's Creed* where the fictional Ezio Auditore de Firenze is a main character surrounded by actual historical people.

Knowing your genre and audience allows you to narrow your focus. For example, steampunk books often rely on the Victorian Era or Industrial Revolution. On the opposite scale, books like *Ender's Game* propel readers to a new age of living and technology where the characters face alien life. Then there are those who want it all, like cyberpunk, a futuristic world with all the pros and cons of the 1980's retro era complete with hot pink and checkered gear. The author decides how much, how little, or how to break the time period (or periods) that lay a foundation for the characters and their world.

One of the most difficult things in this process is creating a timeline for a book or even series. I do this often in my work, and I have no idea why I torture myself—you should decide if you need this. If so, you have to decide if the timeline is for the world or for the character. Often, timelines designed for a world tend to be for an epic novel (100,000 or more words) or to nurture a series of some kind. If this is for a character, you will need to cherry-pick what will push and pull the plot best for the reader and development.

In *Romasanta*, readers follow his life from one century to the next. Sometimes, the story skips over not just years, but decades of his lifespan. Why? Because no one wants to read chapter after chapter of the same content—a man gone feral, eating everything and everyone in sight. Granted, *Romasanta* is book two in a series that already established an initial line from BC to present day. As each book unfolds, readers get more details in the timeline, seeing how events in the past are rippling into the present-day situation.

In *Star Wars*, viewers see a similar large-scale span. The story begins with one generation and fades in and out of the next, seeing how choices made at the beginning still influence the current state of the characters and even the universe. Other timelines are tighter, smaller even. For example, *PS I Love You* has a shorter timeline, one that covers from when a couple meets until she meets a new love. During the story, readers hit points of high emotion with the main character that take them back to a past point on that timeline and let them visit in a short flashback. There are several ways to incorporate a timeline, but the key is be consistent and know there should always be a rippling effect scene somehow.

Here are a few notable examples of how the time period can influence the story, even when traveling through space and time. *Vikings* does a wonderful job bringing the past to life with some accuracy, action, and drama. If you want to see mixing at its best, *Hitchhiker's Guide to the Galaxy* brings the present day into a foreign, alien world. The Japanese animation *Cowboy Bebop* brings the present day into the future like Netflix's *Altered Carbon*. You can also shift the past in your story like *The Man in the High Castle*, an alternate history in which the Allies lose World War II.

A fantastic way to fold your chosen timeline into the mix is pivoting on a major event or invention. Use this change in a way that directly affects something in your story, whether characters, world, or plot. One of my favorite historical books, *Gaijin* by James Clavell, utilizes this tactic constantly throughout the book. From the Yokohama fires to the complications of new nations staking a claim or trading favors to one of many factions, every detail impacts the characters or plot and is a vital part of the world.

Thinking about the time period will breathe life into the setting of your story, enhancing the characters and situations. Planning this way helps you push the story hard right or left when you struggle with a plotline or need the characters to go in a different direction. Don't underestimate the usefulness of establishing key timeline events.

One of my own books leaned hard on this aspect; for *Judgment* in the Tattooed Angels Trilogy, I cherry-picked real disasters as the background for epic battles between the elements of Life and Death. It was a great way to show the impact of their powers not only on themselves or against each other, but on the world around them. I picked events by relying on research to help grasp the moment, then simply plugged in my characters to see how this could drive my plot forward. One of my favorite moments, though startling and gruesome, is in Chapter 14 ("Shadow of the Sun" from *Judgment*) when I used the 1772 drought in India, a morbid experience many British soldiers captured in their journals. I wanted to recreate that and give the reader Talib's (under the alias of Tim here) own firsthand experience as he seeks an out of control element of Light:

"It's true. These poor lads living here haven't seen rain in four years now." A grim expression crossed Henry's face. "When they go back, I try to send children with them. To see men and women suffer is nothing compared to seeing what these young ones face. Most are abandoned, parents dead or no longer able to feed them. You'll see, if you can stomach it, Tim."

"Are we headed for the Doab region?" He could feel the pulse of power pull at him. This was the cause of the drought; being so close now, he could no longer doubt it. "Or is it a lost cause?"

"Unfortunately, we'll be headed there." Wiping sweat from his brow, Talib watched Henry pencil something in his journal. "I haven't been there myself, just yet... not that deep into the mess."

"I see you've been recording what you see?" Furrowing his brow, he patted the man on the back. "I pray your written words do not haunt you as much as the nightmares this place will give you."

"You're a frightening man to talk to at times, Tim." Grunting, Henry put away the journal and they marched on.

It took weeks before they came across a village that still had living people on its streets. To say they were surviving would be a sad lie to comfort you in the decaying landscape. They had passed trenches of dead bodies. Worse, they watched a dying man march himself to one and fall in, dead before hitting the pile. Sickening twists knotted Talib's stomach as he slid down the side of the trench. Catching up to the rolling body, he felt for the man's pulse, knowing it was gone, the dead man's face bearing a smile to be free. The lions in the desert had been far more forgiving than the sun in this place.

They found themselves in a small town, once vibrant with activity judging by the abandoned wagons and merchant stalls. Packs of dogs, as thin as the people with starvation, watched and took account of the living. It was sickening to see the frail skin-and-bone appearance of the natives. Their grotesque physical conditions, starved and malnourished, made them appear inhuman. A dog approached a man leaning against a wall, sniffing at him, drool dribbling from its lips. Tensing, Talib watched, unsure of what he was about to witness. An excited yelp made the rest of the pack pause. A slight wag of the yelper called them back to where he still

stood. Like vultures, they circled around the dying man, patient. They waited for him to pass on before relieving him of the little flesh he retained. Talib could only assume they were too weak to take down a victim who might fight back.

"They pick them clean in two days, if that." Henry's voice cracked, tears fighting to be set lose at the edge of his eyelids. "But that's not the worst of it, Tim."

"It seems the dogs have some respect for those still alive, even if to our eyes he seems dead already." Swallowing, he pulled the scarf farther over his nose. The decaying dead around him reminding him of the smell of bodies from the Black Plague in London so long ago. "So many dead and lying on the road, the fields... wherever they fall."

"Y-yes. Bedrest cannot heal or relieve the hunger that is eating them alive." Henry's shoulders tensed, and he nodded at the shambling remains of a young woman who worked her way toward them. "She's got a little one, I bet..."

The woman made it to where they stood, her skeletal fingers gripping Talib's uniform. "Please, sir! I will sell my child for a rupee! For food! Water!"

ACTIVITY: TIMELINE ASSESSMENT

Date or Year	Major Event	Major Invention	Character	World	Plot

PROJECT TITLE: _____ GENRE: _____

ACTIVITY: Timeline Assessment

Date or Year	Major Event	Major Invention	Character	World	Plot

PROJECT TITLE: _____ GENRE: _____

ACTIVITY: TIMELINE ASSESSMENT

Date or Year	Major Event	Major Invention	Character	World	Plot

ACTIVITY: TIMELINE ASSESSMENT

Date or Year	Major Event	Major Invention	Character	World	Plot

PROJECT TITLE: _____ GENRE: _____

ACTIVITY: TIMELINE ASSESSMENT

Date or Year	Major Event	Major Invention	Character	World	Plot

ACTIVITY: TIMELINE ASSESSMENT

Date or Year	Major Event	Major Invention	Character	World	Plot

ETHNICITY · LANGUAGE · HISTORY · BELIEF

CULTURE LOADING...

Culture

How do we know what is and isn't normal? Let me put it this way... you're at a new school, and you notice everyone takes a sip from a certain water fountain before going to first period. When you fail to do this, you endure a day of dirty looks, and no one will talk to you. You watch for a few days, but still don't comply and get treated badly. At last, you follow the weird custom, and the people, the culture of the school, changes. For the first time in over a week, they say hi to you and explain the drink is a way to keep illness from spreading because that fountain contains healing waters.

BAM! Totally made that up on the fly, but culture gives meaning and spirituality to the world and characters you've built. Culture doesn't always need meaning or a straight connection. It's completely ok fi your characters and readers are discovering the new customs and culture at the same time. In fact, using this technique of introducing a culture can greatly increase reader immersion. There's not a place on this planet that doesn't have some unique mannerisms, customs, religion, social tendencies, government, laws, language, and even trade. Many of these are influenced first by the geography, then by the time period, and next by the people who create the culture. We can look through history for ideas and even build our own like the Sith Lords and Jedi Masters before us. Granted, that doesn't mean we can't use the existing framework. Just do so with respect.

A great example of how even a culture can shift as time passes is the Roman Empire. When they first started out, they aimed to convert the conquered tribes and people to practice Roman mythology by copy/pasting their deities into slots under mainly Hades and Zeus. When the time came and a Roman Emperor of Christian beliefs came into power, the Roman Empire had to keep this mechanism working. Thus, the saints were born with Zeus replaced by Saint Elijah, both using thunder when to invoke a fear of God's punishment in many ways.

Cultures sometimes share similar aspects, for example both Ancient Greek and Celtic mythology contain Apollo, though the first known versions were created completely independent of one another. The reason we know more about the Greek versions, and later the adopted Sun God variant, is due to the fact these were heavily recorded in writing. Celtic belief system on the other hand relied on dryads to sing and oral traditions to maintain their stories and customs. Both of these lasted through the time, though one more recorded than the other over how they handled passing on their religion and belief system.

In short, evaluate how you intend to build your cultures and how they sustain themselves. Do the worship in the home, at a faerie ring, or a temple of some kind? Are their individuals in charge of maintaining the customs and practices? This goes deeper than a variant of clergymen, but governing officials, class systems, ranks in a militant society and more. In the video game series, *Dragon Age*, players realize the great empire of elves has fallen into slavery. With being a complete opposite element than most mainstream fantasy genre, this became a jarring and invigorating aspect to the game. Even more so when a player chose to create an elf character and had to overcome tribulations their lower class status in multiple situations. Culture can create depth, unique experiences, and agency to the worlds within your stories.

ACTIVITY: DEFINING BACKBONE OF CULTURES

Culture	Location	Describe People	Skills/Trades	Main Import/Exports

ACTIVITY: DEFINING BACKBONE OF CULTURES

Culture	Location	Describe People	Skills/Trades	Main Import/Exports

PROJECT TITLE: _____   GENRE: _____

ACTIVITY: DEFINING BACKBONE OF CULTURES

Culture	Location	Describe People	Skills/Trades	Main Import/Exports

ACTIVITY: DEFINING BACKBONE OF CULTURES

Culture	Location	Describe People	Skills/Trades	Main Import/Exports

ACTIVITY: DEFINING BACKBONE OF CULTURES

Culture	Location	Describe People	Skills/Trades	Main Import/Exports

ARCHITECTURE

As cultures develop, they view the world around them in different ways. I adore looking at ruins of ancient cities, wondering what life must have been like in those times. The mosaics of Oplontis and Pompeii show cities known for their bathhouses and luxuries. The ruins today tell us that even in ancient times, these places served as tourist spots. In cold regions, limited shelter made creativity and mobility a must. The methods used by nomads to build and break down their huts and tents showcase a simpler level of architecture.

Comparing Japanese Shinto temples to those of the Mayan's greatest, Chichen Itza, how they were built, why they were built, how they were used, and the way they interacted with their environment vary greatly. Shinto temples provided a way to connect to the deities of the land and often had a spiritually imbued object protected and hidden. Meanwhile, the Mayans used that temple to speak to the people like a megaphone, and at times, blood sacrifices would rain down its steps to appease their deities.

Buildings and holy temples alone do not determine how readers digest a world; smaller things like statues can also be critical. In today's world, superstitions can be seen in different areas. In Louisiana, houses might have thirteen pennies or coins embedded in the porches and front steps. Why? The *rougarou* (swamp werewolf) can't count that high, thus can't enter the home. What is the creature after? Children who didn't fulfill their Catholic duties, of course! These coins are a great example of culture influencing architecture in some interesting ways.

My grandfather notoriously needed a shed for all the different types of crops he harvested; he also enabled Granny's 36 "pet" cats to keep the pests away. Why? Because they kept the rats out! The sheds certainly made the architecture of his mini-culture farmer life seem like visiting a foreign country to my young eyes. Architecture reflects culture; the inhabitants of your world influence every aspect of your world, big or small, whether progressive or traditional.

Elsewhere, statues or guardians abound. My husband's grandfather was a crystal enthusiast, placing certain types in specific areas of the house to encourage good health and fortune while warding against evil. A house decorated this way influences the way visitors perceive the space, and remember, your readers are visitors when they first encounter the world of your story. From there, your characters can make sure readers know to feel at home among these new norms as they explore other areas in your story.

I highly encourage collecting magazines, saving clippings, or creating a Pinterest board to help build a visual guide. Covering the distinctions between Notre-Dame de Paris and St. Mary's Cathedral in Edinburgh can make a world of difference to a reader. Both are gothic in design with towers and huge round stained-glass pieces above the front entrance, but their locations are quite different, and even the people who live in and near them can change the perception of the architecture.

OBJECTS

Access to objects can be a deal breaker. Depending on geography, time period, and culture, you may have limited access to the things your characters use such as weapons, tools, clothing, transportation, household items, special equipment, and more. For example, in the Victorian Era, you would have access to Dead Charlotte charms, creating art from dead people's hair, collecting one's tears in tiny jar, and even taking selfies with the recently deceased via tintypes.

Your time period can limit clothing options, guns, electronics, and more. You can't write a 1980's big-hair band romance with cell phones. Well, you can, but the Motorola DynaTAC was a giant brick launched in 1983 with a whole thirty minutes of talk time before dying. Not sold? Then keep in mind it was a foot long and weighed two and half pounds for the mere price tag of $4,000. Definitely want that in the story! Anyhow, there can be some deal breakers, but in the end, these challenges may help you think outside the box and add in some authentic elements.

If you are writing a Wild West story, and you want them to fly some place commercially, that is still doable (in the later years), though the first planes were scary looking— like wicker chairs inside a wooden frame covered in sheets kind of way. Don't let your cowboy smoke on that flight! In short, you can discover great things by asking the right questions and double-checking when things were discovered or invented.

Connect this research to your Timeline Assessment because both can have huge push and pull on how the story unfolds. Again, the arrangement of these subsections builds off the previous parts. You can't have a bricklaying culture living in huts of mud and grass or have marble buildings in a culture who are pre-carpentry. The tools of these cultures and their environments decide which is more feasible. If they live in a forest area, chances are they are skilled in carpentry and thus skilled lumberjacks. On that same note, they are most likely skilled gatherers and hunters. Knowing that much, you can safely assume they have axes, bows, woven baskets, and log cabins.

Ah, but the question that lies here is what you want your characters to have and be able to have. I usually make a list of what is possible and what is impossible but wanted, then consider how to make that happen. Add aspects of time travel, alien or deity advanced technology, magic, or even blend custom worlds as seen in cyberpunk, steampunk, and alternate history. In the end, it's your story, but be mindful that everything connects to everything else. You have to convince both your characters and readers why this object matters and has the right to exist.

ACTIVITY: Object Want List

Object	Possible or Impossible	Why You Need it	How? Make it happen!

PROJECT TITLE: _____ **GENRE:** _____

ACTIVITY: OBJECT WANT LIST

Object	Possible or Impossible	Why You Need it	How! Make it happen!

ACTIVITY: OBJECT WANT LIST

Object	Possible or Impossible	Why You Need it	How! Make it happen!

ACTIVITY: OBJECT WANT LIST

Object	Possible or Impossible	Why You Need it	How! Make it happen!

PROJECT TITLE: _____ GENRE: _____

ACTIVITY: OBJECT WANT LIST

Object	Possible or Impossible	Why You Need it	How! Make it happen!

PROJECT TITLE: _____   **GENRE:** _____

ACTIVITY: Object Want List

Object	Possible or Impossible	Why You Need it	How! Make it happen!

BACKGROUND AMBIENCE

As a complete nerd about foreshadowing, I think background is one of the more useful tools for tying your world and plot together while engaging readers. For example, having the news on a television or radio, reading the newspaper headlines, or hearing town criers can seed a lot. *Titanic* had some great background elements happening at all times with how the people interacted outside the focal point of the two main characters. The snapshot of the musicians playing as the ship goes down set a tone in that panicked moment that said "no hope."

Fantasy books lean on this element a lot, not only to foreshadow but to establish the state of society in places. When a group of heroes enters a bustling town and market, all seems well. If the next town over is shutting doors and locking windows, something bad has happened or will be happening shortly. It goes back to that ghost story fallback of "it was a dark and stormy night!" You can push readers to know how to feel about the world via the characters, but also by how the world is described. Dystopian novels do this well. There is always this dark, unforgiving background pressure of the world against the character in the tone of how the world is described in the narrative.

Don't hesitate to return to the other sections and worksheets to help you decide on the best way to tackle this.

A place can have been a certain way, but if the characters are arriving in a time of war, turmoil, or celebration, then the experience and perception of the place will change drastically. You can play with options and take advantage of culture in this way or use the seasons or geography to influence the activity of a place. The mackerel season is in peak time versus the peak of winter darkness. How many people and the type of activities down to the clothing worn can shift drastically within the same location.

MECHANICS

Here's where my game development side inspired how I see the writing world. Every book, movie, show, and game has core rules or mechanics. One of my favorite episodes of *Extra Credits* is when they discuss whether a game mechanic can tell a story using *Missile Command* as the example. In short, yes, it can. I believe we can't tell any story without some laws, rules, or mechanics to help keep the world, plot, and characters consistent.

Most stories start with some basics such as the laws of nature. If the wood is wet, you can't light it for campfire. Instead, a fire needs a dry log; dead wood will go up like nobody's business. If you are writing a modern piece, the mechanics are built into your readers. This includes knowing that when Tommy runs across the busy highway, chances are he's going to get hit by a car or cause the biggest pile up New York City has ever seen.

Speculative fiction, on the other hand, gets to break or at least bend the rules a lot. Most magic-based worlds are influenced by the real world. *Avatar: The Last Airbender* is a great example with water trumping fire, earth against wind, and so on. The magic depends on how these elements work in our real world and give readers some understanding of the mechanics of the world. In other examples, magic users have mana and can only use so much. Roleplaying games often limit the number of spells a character can cast based on their level or magic experience.

This doesn't mean the mechanics can't create loopholes. In The Cedric Series, the characters make it clear there is a thing called Gaea's Law. It's a magic spell that keeps her children from turning on one another, and if they do, they are punished threefold. Granted, this doesn't mean all the monsters and magical beings in the world are under this restriction, just a majority within a certain realm. Again, mechanics can be as simple as vampires having to drink blood and werewolves turning only on a full moon. We've been seeing age-old story laws for a long time.

Mechanics are harder to develop and involve more imagination to create something unique. If you're trying to be historically or culturally accurate, then you need to add rules YOU can't break to stay on point with your chosen time, place, and cultures. Adding mechanics is a great way to keep your story consistent. Think of the complications found in the world of *Harry Potter* involving magic or even in *The Lord of the Rings* on how the cultures function.

ACTIVITY: LAYING DOWN THE GROUND RULES

Label	Rule or Mechanic	Plot, World, &/or Character	Purpose	Loopholes

ACTIVITY: LAYING DOWN THE GROUND RULES

Label	Rule or Mechanic	Plot, World, &/or Character	Purpose	Loopholes

ACTIVITY: LAYING DOWN THE GROUND RULES

Label	Rule or Mechanic	Plot, World, &/or Character	Purpose	Loopholes

ACTIVITY: LAYING DOWN THE GROUND RULES

Label	Rule or Mechanic	Plot, World, &/or Character	Purpose	Loopholes

PROJECT TITLE: _____ GENRE: _____

ACTIVITY: Laying Down the Ground Rules

Label	Rule or Mechanic	Plot, World, &/or Character	Purpose	Loopholes

ACTIVITY: LAYING DOWN THE GROUND RULES

Label	Rule or Mechanic	Plot, World, &/or Character	Purpose	Loopholes

CONCLUSION

These are just some core sections to help build your world—the framework supporting your characters and the story you want to tell. Depending on your genre and aim, some of these will be easier to answer while others will elude you. Not every author takes the time to build the world, especially if your story unfolds in the existing world. Relying on research to create new planets, worlds, or even visiting the places of the past can give readers something tangible. When you add your plot and characters into the mix, you provide a vehicle as well as personal experience to what is happening, anchoring readers to the world through the eyes, thoughts, and experiences of a single character or cast of characters.

Be mindful of how a location and time period interact with one another. Clashes here can derail the efforts elsewhere and skew the process. For example, in historical fiction, a desert location today may have been tropical in the past or even underwater. In fact, a city may have gone by a different name, under different influences or rulers, or not even exist yet. Double-checking these elements against one another can catch inaccurate information. You want to add a car, but your timeline says it's not invented for another hundred years, so you need to dive deeper in what common transportation was for the time.

Perhaps consider changing your character's social class to gain access to more objects and so on. Historical fiction pulls a heavier weight in being accurate. I recommend reading Elizabeth Kostova's *The Historian* or even James Clavells' work, *Gai-jin* or *Tai-pan* set in historical Japan and China. They both include large fictional aspects but keep true to the places and time they are living in.

If you are writing a fantasy or science fiction work, be sure to get yourself a notebook or keep an electronic file to keep all your worldbuilding notes. Unlike the previous two genres, contemporary/urban and historical, you must build most of the world, its people, and mechanics from scratch. Don't expect that you can keep it all straight in your memory, especially after multiple stories in that world. The Cedric Series may cross into the urban fantasy realm at times, but the several sketchbooks and files on my computer show that worldbuilding continues. This doesn't mean I need to declare what each mechanic or worldbuilding aspect is nor explain why and how. All an author needs is a checklist to make sure we are consistent and accurate with our creation.

ACTIVITY: HOME AND BEYOND LOCATIONS

	Home	Place	Place	Place
Geography				
Time Period				
Culture				
Architecture				
Objects				
Ambience				
Mechanic/Laws				

ACTIVITY: HOME AND BEYOND LOCATIONS

	Home	Place	Place	Place
Geography				
Time Period				
Culture				
Architecture				
Objects				
Ambience				
Mechanic/Laws				

ACTIVITY: HOME AND BEYOND LOCATIONS

	Home	Place	Place	Place
Geography				
Time Period				
Culture				
Architecture				
Objects				
Ambience				
Mechanic/Laws				

ACTIVITY: HOME AND BEYOND LOCATIONS

	Home	Place	Place	Place
Geography				
Time Period				
Culture				
Architecture				
Objects				
Ambience				
Mechanic/Laws				

ACTIVITY: HOME AND BEYOND LOCATIONS

	Home	Place	Place	Place
Geography				
Time Period				
Culture				
Architecture				
Objects				
Ambience				
Mechanic/Laws				

CHARACTER RESEARCH

As a character-driven writer, I have to confess this type of research is my favorite. It inspires me the most and often bleeds into my research for plot and world. That's okay! The same happens to worldbuilders and plot writers alike. I lose myself diving from one resource to the next when creating a character, especially for The Cedric Series. It may seem silly, but you can pull so many things into your character—both strengths and flaws.

To whom does the story belong?

I ask myself this question often. A common complaint of writer's block is that a writer has a character make a decision the writer would make, but not the decision the character would make. In this situation, you have to backtrack, find where you made this mistake, and rip it all out. Doing character research is a great way to remind yourself whose story you are sharing with readers. However, choosing the main character can sometimes be tricky. Depending on your genre, this choice can have reader expectations that complicate your aim.

- A single character
- Main character and love interest
- Cast of characters on a quest

Fantasy often features a group of characters that may complicate your attempts to write an intimate storyline. A common formula for most romances is to split the narrative between the main character and love interest.

It's a fun way to reveal internal conflicts and external perspectives—and can be extremely helpful for comedies. Other literary works latch onto a single character in third person point-of-view (he, she, her, him) or even first-person point of view (me, you, I, myself). Granted, this doesn't mean your research here will help you decide the best way to tell your story. That's a later discussion.

Does research really influence character design?

You have no idea! Elisabeth Bathory is a great example of an exhausted research vein. More infamous for her nickname as the Blood Countess, she has influenced the vampire and paranormal genre for centuries. Yes, even *Carmilla* and *Dracula* have some hints referring back to her dark history and desire to bathe in blood. She wanted to be immortal but also young and beautiful forever. Another example would be Nikola Tesla. Appearing on movie screens played by a wide variety of actors, Tesla maybe known historically as Thomas Edison's rival, but his influence can be seen in stories such as *The Prestige, Murdoch Mysteries, Fragments of Olympus*, and many more.

As the author, you choose how to apply the research to a character.

The stories don't have to be explicitly historical fiction or even focused on the life of the historical character. In the series *Penny Dreadful*, where paranormal fiction is inspired by literary works such as *Frankenstein, Dracula, Dr. Jekyll and Mr. Hyde,* and *The Picture of Dorian Grey,* the historically identifiable Joan of Arc appears but in a completely fictional capacity. Not once did the story mention anything historical, only referred to her backstory as her past experiences. Don't be afraid to twist and bend history where needed so you can create the perfect plot and world.

HISTORY

As I pointed out above, history can influence how characters develop. The research here gives agency and support on how feasible an idea actually can be. For murder mystery and detective noir authors, research can explore famous cases like Jack the Ripper and the Zodiac Killer. Influential historical events can also inspire your characters.

I mentioned Joan of Arc, but pandemics like the Black Plague or even the New England Vampire Epidemic are often overlooked. The latter was caused by the increase of tuberculosis combined with poor sanitation practices. Families buried victims, assumed dead from consumption, only for them to wake later. Soon, rumors spread that the dead were coming back to feed on the living, giving birth to an American vampire scare—and Bram Stoker was here in America with an acting troupe at the time, and when he went home to England with all those amazing newspaper clippings, he wrote *Dracula.*

dynamics of "modern living" during his time period. *Oliver Twist, Tale of Two Cities,* and *Great Expectations* all put readers in complicated situations with a level of prey and predator, especially regarding class systems. Children pickpocketed like champs on the streets of London, the rich preyed on the unfortunate and naïve, and clever criminals often employed or bullied child labor on some level.

Even fantasy work with its share of kings and queens draws inspiration from real life monarchies. Whether you want to revive the Persian Empire or build your own mixture of English-monarch-meets-ancient-Chinese-emperor, you have full control. This is your story, but you need to make the character aware of the dynamics and give them a status in this culture you've created. The reader experiences the world through the character's experiences. Through your character's emotions, readers learn how they should feel about the world, the plot points, and the other people in this world.

- ✐ Geographical
  - ✎ Cerdanya and the nearby Lepers Colony were indeed places in the 12th century and central hubs of trade and the ill. (https://en.wikipedia.org/wiki/Cerdanya)

- ✐ History/Geographical
  - ✎ Historical version of Romasanta grew up in the same Spain/France region where Cerdanya once was located.

- ✐ Architectural/History
  - ✎ As the story progresses and the surroundings change, the buildings and the background characters show the passing of time best to express Romasanta's immortality.

MYTHOLOGY

Most of my work and character research pulls from folklore, superstition, urban legends, fairy tales, and more importantly, mythology. There are so many variations, and tales of Hercules, Apollo, and Zeus have been told for ages. This doesn't mean you can't put an original spin on one or tell the story in a new way. I often dive hard and deep for the foundation of my characters while trying to stay within the don't and Want Lists for my worldbuilding.

A great example of putting a new spin on an age-old tale is Madeline Miller's *Song of Achilles*, which takes the story from Patroclus and reveals a blossoming romance between the two heroes. The Achilles legend has been around for centuries and has been re-imagined many times, including *Troy* starring Brad Pitt as Achilles. Much like the fairy tales *Cinderella* and *Snow White*, these stories continue to capture the audience while delivering amazing characters.

Even Stephenie Meyer's *Twilight* mingles fairy and vampire lore. You can apply your research to your characters as you wish. The world will never forget sparkling vampires, and in some ways, Meyer changed how our modern culture sees these creatures. Even more modern monster tales using zombies vary: some are started by disease while others are a result of an alien invasion. Whatever the cause, how the characters live and survive changes and even the zombies can act differently.

✒ Mythology

   🖎 Fenrir is part of Romasanta for a good portion of Book 2. He is from Norse mythology. I dove into that lore and used Romasanta as the "Stone" in which Fenrir is "chained" as my concept. Again, I didn't feel the need to use all of the lore, but often used them metaphorically, especially involving the complications I wanted for Romasanta's origin story. (https://en.wikipedia.org/ wiki/Fenrir)

✒ Superstition

   🖎 Romanians and many medieval superstitions believed someone who died with unfinished business would come back as a werewolf or skin changer. Many sources reference how the bitten/clawed victim would return an undead who fed on the living.

✒ Mythology

   🖎 Apollo had some vague lore mentioning a relation to wolves, even House of Wolves and King of Arcadia. That was more than enough for me to add him into the mix. For example, Romasanta shares a lot from Apollo such as a twin sister named Artemis and a lover named Daphne. (https://en.wikipedia.org/wiki/Apollo)

✒ Urban Legend

   🖎 In Haiti, there is a belief that werewolves like digging up bodies to eat them and steal their valuables. You see a glimpse of this in a very important moment between Romasanta and a younger Cedric. (*Encyclopaedia of Gods, Monsters & Legend* by Carol Rose)

     ✒ Folklore

       🖎 Black Dog/Black Wolf hunted those who had done Mother Nature wrong or were ill-natured. (*Encyclopaedia of Gods, Monsters & Legend* by Carol Rose; *Dictionary of Mythology from A to Z* by JA Coleman)

     ✒ Legend

       🖎 Romulus and Remus were twins raised by a She-wolf. SPOILER: It was only natural for their father also be wolf-like and a twin! Rhea, their mother, had insisted their father was Mars and in some weird variants even Apollo. There were a lot of discrepancies, which only gave me more room to add my own flair and imagination. (https:// en.wikipedia.org/wiki/ Romulus_and_Remus)

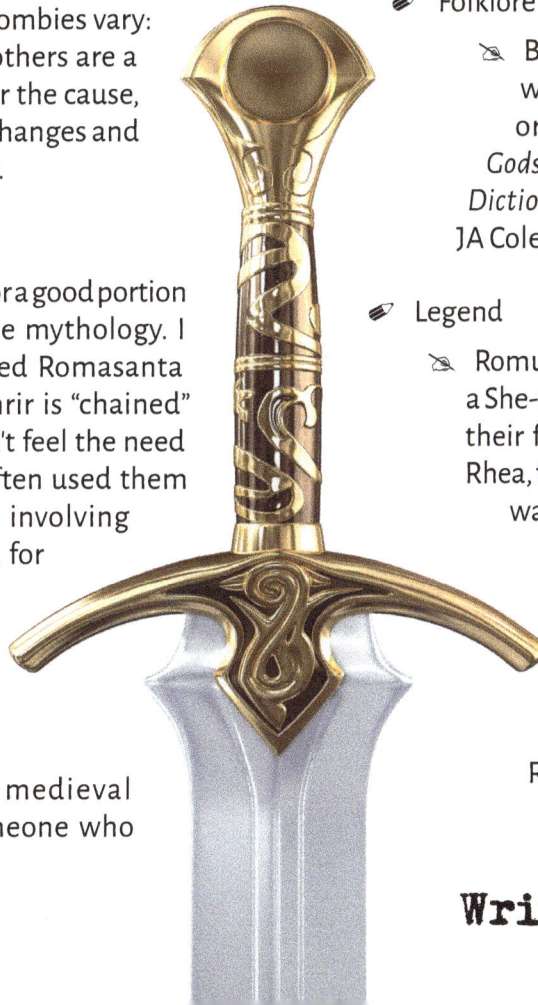

PEOPLE

Whether you plan on following the path less travelled or not, there is much to be learned from people. This doesn't mean you have to dive into Joan of Arc or the life of Marco Polo. You can draw influence from the people in your everyday life. Don't be afraid to add a character or two who remind you of relatives, friends, enemies, acquaintances, and beyond. Often in my youth, I would sit on a bench at the local mall and people-watch. It's okay—as writers, we can call it research as long as we're not stalker-level creepy.

Don't forget that adding an Easter egg or writing a fan into your story can be a great prize or exclusive. It's a wonderful way to invest others in your book and build excitement for the book launch. People can really make a difference in a story. It's like watching *Always Be My Maybe* when Keanu Reeves makes his cameo. Having a character declare "I punched John Wick" is a great way to pull people into a story. Don't be afraid to pull in earnest thoughts, feelings, and actions no matter how strange they seem.

Often, romantic comedies use internal dialogue to showcase panic while they feigning nonchalance externally. These moments, like the famous trip and fall in the movie *Miss Congeniality*, says volumes about the character themselves and how readers can relate. Even when historical fiction replays a battle, stories can show the pain, fear, and bravery in more intimate ways than a history book.

Fact is stranger than fiction

This rings true, especially when you start to do research on people in history. Whether you are discovering some gruesome dark entity or discovering an unkillable man in World War II, you will find things which seem impossible. If research doesn't prove helpful, at least here it can give you agency to put that idea into motion. Picking elements from several sources is a great way to create your very own *Frankenstein's* monster of your own. As you lay them to paper, using plot points and having them interact with your world, they begin to breathe and bleed on your page.

✒ Person

   ✎ His name is inspired by Manuel Romasanta, a man who went on trial for being a serial killer and confessed to being a werewolf. Ironically, his mother was superstitious and believed in many Romanian-based versions. He was also an accomplished farmer, merchant, and soap maker, which I also brought into the story. (https://en.wikipedia.org/wiki/Manuel_Blanco_Romasanta)

ART & CREATIVE WORK

Statues, cave paintings, art, and even writing can inspire other stories and storytellers. As I pointed out before, much of popular mythology is told through creative work on the screen or in the pages of a book. Circling back to a prior example, *Penny Dreadful* is a great example of using public domain creative works from the 1800's and making something new and exciting. It romanticizes those dreadful stories once bought for a penny in the streets of London.

Tall tales and imagery of them can also be influential as seen in the Disney film *Tall Tale* where a boy finds himself in the company of American tales, including John Henry, Pecos Bill, Paul Bunyan, and even Calamity Jane. The interesting thing here is the history tied into it, the industrialization of the Wild West. In fact, Calamity Jane may have some tall tales, but she was indeed a cowgirl in her time famous for bringing trouble.

Plenty of stories have been inspired by famous works of art or even art in general. In Jim Henson's *Mirror Mask*, a troubled teen explores a world of her art creations. Robin Williams stars in *What Dreams May Come*, finding himself in paintings and magical worlds as he searches for his wife's soul. In 2003, a movie based on the book *Girl with a Pearl Earring* placed a story behind one of the most famous paintings by Johannes Vermeer under the same name. Again, people real and fictional can inspire amazing tales, and as an author, you can explore the most important question:

What if?

Your portrayal of the people you use doesn't have to be accurate. Be mindful of the genre and audience you are writing for, though. Historical readers are going to be less forgiving on the fictional and inaccuracy of certain elements. Alternative history and fantasy readers will enjoy breaking traditional molds and venturing down the unexplored paths. Be aware of this as you do your research, and keep track of the sources you are pulling from.

- Artwork and Statues
  - Apollo and tales of Daphne have featured in a wide variety of painting, sculptures, and even pottery. Often Apollo is carrying a bow and wearing a wolfskin.

- Creative Work/Legends
  - Many resources start off as simply folklore and legends. Apollo has stories from Gallic, Celtic, Roman, and even Ancient Greek times. It took a lot of time to place timestamps and figure out which were the oldest. (My findings here: http://www.scififantasynetwork.com/celtic-apollo-greek-apollo/)

OBJECTS

Yes, objects are part of worldbuilding when considering time period, but don't underestimate the power of objects on your story overall. One item can wield enormous power over how a plot unfolds as well as affect characters internally and externally. In *The Lord of the Rings*, readers know how much that single ring impacts the world, plot, and characters. It destroys lives and brings chaos to an entire world. Readers understand how important it is for Frodo Baggins to be the bearer of such a dangerous object.

Not all objects have to be malicious. For example, the *Sisterhood of the Travelling Pants* series focuses on a magic pair of jeans. The story primarily focuses on the character growth of a group of girls coming of age, but the plot device and tool at hand is simply a pair of jeans. This object links the girls together and gives readers something relatable.

Another element to consider is the power or influence items may have on a character. *Indiana Jones* and *Tomb Raider* rely on the characters' ambition to find the impossible item. Sometimes, items can be enchanted to aid our characters in navigating the plot and world. Often these elements are great ways to turn a story in a new direction without it feeling forced. J.K. Rowling's *Harry Potter* series uses objects like brooms, amulets, journals, pictures, wands, and more to move the story forward. At every turn, there is an opening for an item with amazing or even unpredictable abilities and magic.

The Man in the Iron Mask features an unknown prisoner who has lived with an iron mask for some time. Not only is this a book by Alexandre Dumas and a movie starring Leonardo DiCaprio, but this story also has some history behind it. This prime example shows how objects and events can link together in some amazing ways. Not only that, but this story of an individual's situation launched a chain of events the world still finds fascinating today.

- Objects
  - Vodka is an important object in my stories. In my research, I found accounts of a new liquor in Cerdanya that met its description and was reportedly received from Lepers. On that note, Lepers were the top producers of potatoes at this time. Also, "vodka" was used for medicine and cleaning wounds, not necessarily as a main drink choice. (http://www.ginvodka.org/history/vodkaHistory.asp)

- Object/Myth/Legend
  - The Eye of Gaea or Philosopher's Stone plays a huge part in Romasanta's destiny. So there was a large mixture of myth and my imagination involved with these items.

ANIMALS

If you haven't read Jack London's *Call of the Wild*, then I highly recommend it. When a main character is an animal, there is a lot of research required. In this particular novel, Jack London combines the current situation and put readers in the body and mind of a dog experiencing it. Kidnapped from his home, Buck has to survive the Alaskan gold rush. Using the dog's voice, London showed the world what was happening in America at the time.

London wasn't the only one taking advantage of animal characters. For ages, authors like Beatrix Potter with the *Tale of Peter Rabbit* and Robert Down with *Watership Down* used animals to tell their stories. Granted, Potter's lighthearted stories are quite the opposite of Down's brutal story, despite both using rabbits as main characters. Morals and social issues come to life in these works, allowing readers to both disconnect and reconnect in unexpected ways. Adding some imagination and research can shake how readers see the events. In *Charlotte's Web*, readers realize that eventually Wilbur will "meat" his end if something amazing doesn't prevent his fate.

These examples are not the only way you can use animals for characters in your story. Instead of having animals as the characters, you can give your knight a trusty steed or give your character an animal companion. *Game of Thrones* uses dire wolves and dragons. In some works, the animals are fictional, but that doesn't mean they don't need some sort of research or notes taken to keep them consistent. Anne McCaffrey's *Dragonriders of Pern* series consistently follows her rules surrounding the creatures she introduces. Both feel familiar but new as readers learn about them through the characters themselves.

Sometimes the animals reflect some part of our main characters, embodying a hidden or suppressed aspect. *I Am Legend* uses the dog to reveal the narrator's experience, this seemingly small detail giving the character a way to voice how he copes, and when things shift, the animal's portrayal, especially on screen, shows it.

In some works, the characters face the animals. In the famous *Jungle Book*, Mowgli will have to face Shere Khan eventually. Rudyard Kipling didn't choose this opponent by chance. During this time, man-eating tigers were feared, and many died attempting to hunt down these beasts. The other animals Mowgli encounters all have a purpose in revealing something about himself, the plot, and the world he calls home compared to the world he needs to call home.

✎ Animal/Myth

  ✐ Because Fenrir is a wolf, a lot of normal wolf-like behavior is added into Romasanta himself.

MEDICAL & MENTAL HEALTH

Another aspect of character research and design is medical and mental health. In The Cedric Series, my characters experience the "ailments of man" which include depression, heartache, anxiety, and so much more. The idea here is that, despite their immortality and power, they still have flaws and mental health to deal with. Often, readers follow as my characters deal with post-traumatic stress disorder caused by war and abuse on epic scales.

If a character makes a mistake or has a flaw on some level, it's okay because this creates a tangible aspect, something similar to the rest of humanity. Readers may enter a story to escape, and some may want to watch characters experience things worse than their own lives, especially in the horror or fantasy genres. Some tales use medical conditions as a core plot point, whether it be a magical curse or an actual condition. A great example of this is *The Fault in Our Stars* by John Green where the main characters all are suffering from some physical condition or cancer. This illness changes how they interact with each other and the world, taking readers down a path they may not recognize.

A book that shook me in middle school was called *The Only Alien on the Planet* by Kristen D. Randle. I picked it up, excited to see a science fiction book, but instead found myself thrown into a story about a boy who wouldn't talk. As the main character befriends this strange boy, readers realize his brother is abusing him, trauma that creates this silence. A book featuring mental or medical aspects as a core element of the character, plot, and world can really speak to readers in ground-shaking ways. Much like Jack London, you can feature a taboo issue and let readers experience it firsthand through your characters and story telling.

If you use known medical and mental health issues, make sure you do the proper research. This is one of the

many times (culture, ethnicity, race, religion and more) you will want a Beta reader or proofreader who can help identify red flags and misconceptions in your depiction. It's not about offending someone—because that may be the aim in some cases—but be sure to representing these in an accurate and respectful way. For example, *The Shape of Water* focuses on a mute main character who, like her non-white coworker, is treated differently in the workplace and by the government. Even her gender and the secondary character's sexuality show the world's merciless cruelty. This story captures several social issues, showing both mental and medical scenarios clashing in a volatile time and situation. This also jars the modern audience into realizing we still have these issues and have yet to overcome them even now.

I can't promise you that thorough research on this aspect is enough to avoid or prevent all whiplash. It's going to happen. Some may see *The Fault in Our Stars* as a gross representation of romanticizing horrible medical situations and cancer. Others may see this piece as a way of declaring "everyone deserves to experience love" and appreciate that message. Meanwhile, I just see it as a tearjerker no different from *PS I Love You* and a chance to give myself an ugly-cry session not related to my own turmoil.

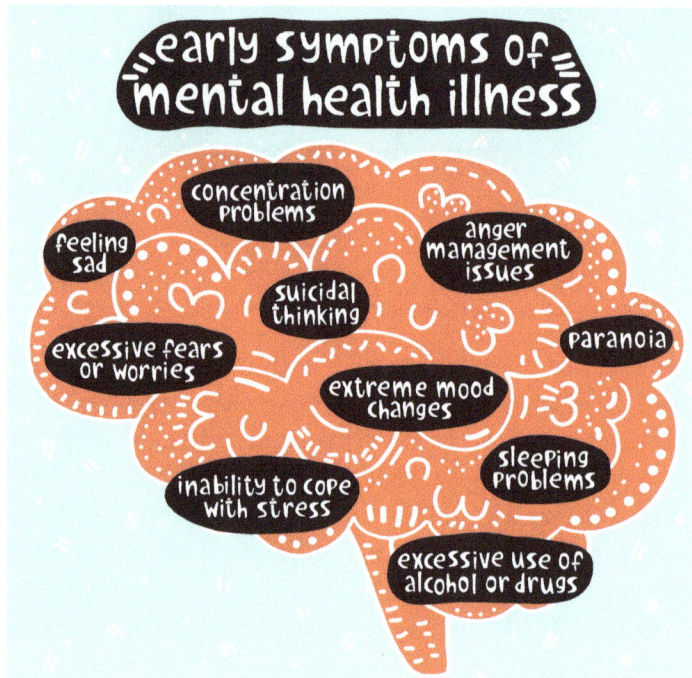

early symptoms of mental health illness

concentration problems · feeling sad · anger management issues · suicidal thinking · excessive fears or worries · paranoia · extreme mood changes · inability to cope with stress · sleeping problems · excessive use of alcohol or drugs

✐ People/Mental Health

 🖎 My research into Emanuel Romasanta revealed a lot about his mental health. At one point, after confessing guilt, a local mental hospital evaluated him. Some of the records show that his mother tried to "cheat the curse" by dressing and treating him as a girl until a doctor intervened when Romasanta was about five.

✎ PTSD, grief, and feral tendencies were all part of the consequences of everything unfolding in this book. I had to do extensive research on this, and the findings influenced how Romasanta would fall into them and pull back out. At one point, Nyctimus and Lillith pull him out, forcing him to face the truth he avoided for centuries.

CONCLUSION

You're probably looking at this list and seeing some ideas bubble. That's good! More importantly, don't tie yourself down to just this list, or even just one of these on here. Mix and match your research, and cherry-pick the things that compliment your story and character's needs. I unmasked Romasanta and exposed the inner workings of all the different research elements used to influence him and his story. Needless to say, I once gave a computer lab full of college students a two-hour lecture on his inner makings which ended in applause. I used a combination of resources to achieve my character research, not stopping at just books and online sites. In fact, I emailed a few experts writing articles I read and sought their input as well.

I know—that's a lot of crazy research tunnels to create *ONE* character. Readers don't grasp all of this information at all when they first meet him in *Cedric: The Demonic Knight*. As *Romasanta: Father of Werewolves* progresses, readers can see how each element flows in and out of the story. Character, plot points, and worldbuilding research begin to overlap, weaving a tapestry of one character's struggles. Some threads establish Romasanta's decisions and skillsets in a situation; others are part of his heritage and drive development that way.

Again, as I've pointed out before, you don't have to reveal, declare, or use all the research for a character. These are tools for the author to create agency and consistency in your work. Don't feel obligated to find a place for all of it. Instead, know that you can keep writing and when a situation unfolds, you can rely on the research to see what they would do. In one scene, Romasanta uses his soapmaking skills to mask his scent from a blind dragon. How he achieves this and the gruesome turn of events really fell back on the research I collected. This wasn't a planned portion, but I had come to a pickle and panicked. How could they sneak into the castle? And the answer was in the soapmaking history of his namesake.

"Let's go build some characters <3 This is my favorite part!"

ACTIVITY: CHARACTER RESEARCH

	Main	Character	Character	Character
History				
Mythology				
People				
Art &Creative Work				
Objects				
Animals				
Medical & Mental				

ACTIVITY: CHARACTER RESEARCH

	Main	Character	Character	Character
History				
Mythology				
People				
Art &Creative Work				
Objects				
Animals				
Medical & Mental				

ACTIVITY: Character Research

	Main	Character	Character	Character
History				
Mythology				
People				
Art &Creative Work				
Objects				
Animals				
Medical & Mental				

ACTIVITY: CHARACTER RESEARCH

	Main	Character	Character	Character
History				
Mythology				
People				
Art &Creative Work				
Objects				
Animals				
Medical & Mental				

ACTIVITY: CHARACTER RESEARCH

	Main	Character	Character	Character
History				
Mythology				
People				
Art &Creative Work				
Objects				
Animals				
Medical & Mental				

PLOT POINTS

Another line of research I do is based on the event or scene I am writing. Often, I do this research in more depth when I start to write that part. These would be key plot points in your story that can twist the story or characters in important ways. As I begin, I often leave myself notes. Most of the information I find builds on my previous character and/or worldbuilding research.

Google, can skin melt?

Writers tend to look like murderers from our internet search history. We ask in-depth questions about what we want to write, diving into newfound resources. We live in a great time for writing because strange questions have been asked before us—and it's easy to find answers online. Granted, it can be intimidating to create something for a scene.

How to hunt a deer...

Some of us capture something we've done, whether diving through the sky or ocean. On the other hand, we may not have firsthand experience, but find ourselves telling the story of a character who is a master at this hunting deer thing. Don't be afraid to look it up, ask a friend, ask an expert, or seek out articles and videos. The more exposure you have on a topic, the more it reflects in your work.

The ground began to shake, the sky blackening as lightning and ash fell upon us.

Not every plot point leans on characters and what they are doing. There are times where things happen in the world or plot that is beyond the character's control, helping the author twist the story's direction. Fun fact: when a volcano starts to erupt, it can cause so much static electricity that it produces lightning. In short, the more we know, the more intensely we can describe the scene. Asking questions produces unique ways for an author to show what is happening.

Shot heard round the world.

Don't be afraid to use every research aspect to your advantage. There have been so many natural and mechanical disasters that you can create one of your own by piecing together what you've uncovered. Also, it's not a coincidence that a lot of historical romances overlap with war on some level. There's a whole genre tied to the Civil War, including the famous *Gone with the Wind*. There is a struggle and wildcard aspect to having the characters live in tumultuous times. The idea that at any moment the dull roar of distant cannons could result in one coming through the window keeps the readers and characters in a constant state of motion.

SKILLS, TRADES & TALENTS

Many characters have a skill, trade, talent, or something similar. Not all of us share these with our characters, but diving into research can help us decribe appropriate habits. This provides a way for us to manipulate a plot point in some amazing ways. Katniss from *The Hunger Games* is a skilled hunter with the bow. This later becomes a weapon and plot device that shifts difficult moments to her favor time and time again. In *Always Be My Maybe*, the idea the two love interests would cross paths seems impossible. That is, until he works as an air conditioner technician for his dad's company—which she hires. These skills open doors in viable ways.

- For example, soap maker, air conditioner contractor, bounty hunter ability to re-assemble a gun, etc.

HISTORICAL

If your characters are involved in a historical event, you can describe the event and your character's involvement with it in some amazing ways. One of my personal favorite authors, James Clavell, does this during a volatile time in China and Japan. Readers feel like they are experiencing a soap opera at times while fictional characters represent the many sides of events at that time. As things unfold, the plot jerks left-and-right as historical events unfold around the characters. From the Yokohama fires to the battles between the Emperor and Shogun, Clavell had large toy box to pull from at any given moment. I recommend making a list of possible events you can pull from, but again, don't feel obligated to use it all. The idea is to use these plot points to inspire you when you get stuck. Mass genocides in even fantasy pieces can have some connections to history.

For example, James Clavell's *Gai-jin* covers the Yokohama fires and how the characters all deal with it differently.

- Unmasking of the "man in the iron mask" holds many possibilities.

NATURAL DISASTERS

Earthquakes, tsunamis, hurricanes, tornadoes, and even plagues are a few of the things that can happen in even fantasy-based worlds. Researching witness accounts gives you ideas of how your character should react to what is going on when you throw them in these scenarios. Whether you capture something on a historical scale or gather data for a fictional event, there are lots of recorded accounts. Even as Helike fell into the sea, major repercussions continued, including the destruction of a huge chunk of the Roman Empire's naval fleet. These plot points don't just change the direction a character is going, but the world and environment on multiple levels. Depending on the time period, you should be seeing evidence of events still echoing in the background or ripples of resulting chain reactions.

✐ For example, Romasanta takes refuge in a lepers' colony. Even though he is immune to this pandemic, watching these people and their struggles as they die affects him.

MECHANICAL DISASTERS

Car crashes, train wrecks, spaceships being sucked into black holes (both a natural and mechanical disaster), building collapses: these are just a few disasters you can research for details. There are videos, photos, and written accounts of folks dying and surviving in a variety of scenarios. Whether you are marooned sailors in the middle of the ocean or trapped in a collapsing building, the situation turns into an unpredictable scenario. It's up to an author whether a character's luck will be good or bad. Just remember the mental and physical health of a character changes during a plot point like this, and the event can create new obstacles including new fears or triggers.

✐ For example, in my novel *Judgment*, Talib is trapped under a collapsed building, and the ordeal of figuring out how to escape causes him (and readers) to question the benefits of immortality in this scenario.

WARTIME CATASTROPHE

War has a plethora of weaponry that pushes the limits of men and machines. A fantasy story may use magic while science fiction may explore the darker side of science—like atomic bombs. The research here can be heartbreaking, so tread lightly. Again, like some of the others, this plot point can scar the characters and world. Ernest Hemingway changed dramatically after World War I, and often those who write about him evaluate how it affected him as a writer and storyteller.

✐ For example, consider the long-term effects of the war in which Harry Potter and friends find themselves.

GOALS

A vague term at first, but this aligns with our expectations for characters as they achieve their goals in the story. The goal may be murder, fighting, learning a new skill, undergoing some sort of character development moment, or any events that pull together in a special way. Often, this is one of the main plot points that peaks at the climax of the story. *Star Wars* does a wonderful job at placing each character's goals in direct conflict with other character goals in the universe. Know that goals can be dark or light; they can even be simultaneously selfish and selfless. Goals reflect who the characters may be as well as how they feel about their world.

✐ For example, Romasanta uses his specialized knowledge to outsmart the dragon, tricking the creature's sensitive nose with soap.

CONCLUSION

None of these are concrete must-haves in the plot of your story. Look at this list a little more loosely than the prior two research types, since your genre and story decide how much of each you will have. For example, the movie *Titanic* centers around a historically famous mechanical disaster. Yet viewers follow two characters who fall in love while on the boat during the disaster of a lifetime. Think about the topics you can research and use this information to connect your event, characters, and world to one another. You should have a sense of overlapping events on occasion—how does it all fit together?

In some cases, you may only pull from two of these categories, like in *Always Be My Maybe*. Use plot points with the skill and trades section in connection with the goals of each character.

ACTIVITY: PLOT POINTS PUSH, PULL, & TWIST (BOP IT!)

	Push	Pull	Twist
Character			
Character			
Character			
World			
World			
World			

ACTIVITY: PLOT POINTS PUSH, PULL, & TWIST (BOP IT!)

	Push	Pull	Twist
Character			
Character			
Character			
World			
World			
World			

ACTIVITY: PLOT POINTS PUSH, PULL, & TWIST (BOP IT!)

	Push	Pull	Twist
Character			
Character			
Character			
World			
World			
World			

ACTIVITY: PLOT POINTS PUSH, PULL, & TWIST (BOP IT!)

	Push	Pull	Twist
Character			
Character			
Character			
World			
World			
World			

ACTIVITY: Plot Points Push, Pull, & Twist (Bop it!)

	Push	Pull	Twist
Character			
Character			
Character			
World			
World			
World			

ACTIVITY: PLOT POINTS PUSH, PULL, & TWIST (BOP IT!)

	Push	Pull	Twist
Character			
Character			
Character			
World			
World			
World			

EXAMPLE FROM ROMASANTA

What good are all the examples and ideas if I can't show you what madness research can create? Below is a section from one of my novels, *Romasanta: Father of Werewolves*. Pay attention to how the details I listed about him (farmer, Fenrir, animal/wolf) come together in this scene. I've walked through Romasanta's design process with you; now it's time for the finished package. I hope this connects the pieces into a solid finale. FYI: Fenrir and Romasanta share a single body here, though they both have the ability to interact with each other.

Fenrir and Romasanta shuddered as they stood over the broken body of Boreas. It reeked, and Nyctimus refused to be near the heap any longer. Shifting back into a man, Romasanta disregarded his clothes. Instead, he grabbed a knife and pot, going to work on the carcass before him. Digging his fingers deep, he removed skin and pulled slabs of fat from Boreas' mutilated body.

What are you doing, Farmer? Fenrir's curiosity vibrated through him as he filled the pot with fat. *Do you aim to consume Boreas? If so, this is not the best part...*

Romasanta shook his head, absorbed in his labor as he poured salt into the pot and set it on hot coals. "I am making tallow, for soap."

Fenrir snorted. *This is no time to bathe, Farmer.*

Chuckling, Romasanta explained his intentions for the tallow. "My dear Fenrir, you humor me at times. I will not be adding flowers to this soap. It serves a different purpose. Instead, I will be adding Boreas' hair and slithers of skin so when I bathe with it, I will be scented the same as he. Did you not tell me Aitvaras has poor eyesight in the day?"

Excitement rattled Fenrir's core. *This is the clever man I have come to envy!*

"You do me too much honor to envy me. I am nothing but a farmer, Fenrir." With the greatest care, Romasanta cut thin, small slivers of Boreas' skin and fur, adding them to the boiling pot of fat. "I am doing this to avoid being burnt alive. If it overwhelms our nose, it will fool him for sure."

Nyctimus crawled closer to Rhea, whispering to her in hopes Romasanta could not hear. "Who in the Gods is he talking to?"

"Fenrir," she beamed, enjoying the interaction between man and beast. "They were cursed to share Romasanta's body."

"How do you know which one you are talking to?" Furrowing his brow, Nyctimus's hazel eyes seemed big against his brown wolf head. "Is there a secret to recognizing the man from the wolf?"

Sighing, Rhea watched as Romasanta hovered over the bowling pot. He removed large chunks of meat as they broke away from the melting fat.

She turned back to Nyctimus with a reply, "You are always talking to both."

Looking over his shoulder, Nyctimus gazed sorrowfully at the cursed naked man at the fire. "And I thought my curse was difficult. I am simply a man who turns into a wolf, but he is two beings..."

Satisfied he had only fat in the pot, Romasanta let it continue to simmer without his aid. Gripping the putrid corpse, he dragged it with him. Nyctimus marveled at the ease with which he shifted from human to werewolf. The entire process was painful as muscles stretched and bones shattered to make room. Anyone who was near them could hear the popping of the forceful metamorphism that took place at incredible speed. Romasanta left them at the fire as he carried the body far away. The strength he had, the numbness from shifting frightening.

RESOURCE TYPES

Research resources come in many shapes and sizes. Some of my best resources are college theses or academic publications written in the early 1900's or older. You should be familiar with internet and books as a primary resource. In today's age, you can search through these materials for keywords and specific names, but there are other methods to get more genuine information not always found in these places. Let's start from easiest to access to the more difficult type to dive into. Know that this is a listing based not only from my experience, but the recommendation and back stories from authors I have encountered in my career to date.

INTERNET

The internet is a great starting point for most research. It can lead you to many of the other resources, but I don't recommend depending on it alone. Venture out and combine this resource with some of the others. A great way to do this is to look at the cited sources and keep tracing it back to the original sources. You may be surprised how often something might be changed or paraphrased in such a way that it doesn't follow the original source at all. This takes a bit of detective work and will often lead you to a different type of resource such as books, experts, and museums.

BOOKS, JOURNALS, & NEWSPAPERS

I still find some of the best stuff hidden in the pages of books. Even my best resources of photos from the Civil War and World War II are on my shelf, not online. A lot of material and research captured here never makes it to the web or internet sources due to special permissions (given only for print sources). Don't underestimate these tomes even in the digital age! And not everything is searchable via the internet. I often seek out 1800's publications and have to download and read these scanned pages to find the interesting content. Many of these sources have been discontinued because no one has attempted to republish them now.

Using a library or college access, you can read journals and newspapers via the internet. Know that your search engine will not find some of these; you will have to login to specific databases and search that system for older content. You can also go to a local library to gain physical access to some of these. With the internet filtering and limiting your results, you may miss a valuable resource. Nothing beats a good old-fashioned book dive, whether at a library, thrift store, or bookstore.

FICTION

This may seem odd, but fictional sources can be very helpful in revealing more about a time period or understanding why something was so popular. For example, the Dead Charlotte charms were based on a popular sonnet at the time titled *Poor Charlotte* (or in a more recent recording, *The Frozen Girl* by Cordelia's Dad). Looking at Grimm's Fairy tales and similar books reveals common fears and accepted morality viewed as important for both children and society. Nursery rhymes even hold a dark realization such as "Ring Around the Rosie." Many of the writers from the 1800's also published books with their resources, and these sometimes show both fictional and historical information.

Non-fiction

My personal favorite resource are collections of mythology or historical events and decades, though I favor those with great photos or illustrations because I'm a visual learner. Having books with photos of the people, events, or items enhances my ability to digest the information and write about it effectively. These sources often generate leads to follow up or unique research topics. Don't be afraid to lean on the older books in this genre. The thrift store can be a sweet place to find old encyclopedia collections as well as old historical books. I once discovered *Military Cultures of the World* in a used bookstore—can't find it anywhere else (it even has a Frankfurt, Germany library stamp—published in 1940!). How cool!

Experts

Call them, email them, go to them, and find them! Never hesitate to reach out to a college professor or the neighbor who's a whiz about something. Some of my most valuable resources have been friends and acquaintances who have hobbies overlapping. Whether consulting Kathy on her American Civil War knowledge or the mother-in-law on rocks and gemstones, someone in your life has a niche. Use it! Remember that asking someone about the very thing they are good at, or experts of, is a compliment. Writers geek out about their stories and so do experts when asked about the things that interest them. They can give insight on how to illustrate something in your world, characters, or story.

Field Trip

Never underestimate the effect of a drive or trip somewhere. This can be harder for someone like me with no funds while writing about Delphi, Greece. But this limitation didn't stop me from looking at travel guides, vacation packages, and similar resources to discover more about visiting Delphi. I asked around and found someone who had been there (lived there)! Also, if you're writing about your hometown or somewhere close you... take that drive! Ask for the local historian or ask for a recommendation of who would be best to ask. Mark Muncy, the author behind *Eerie Florida*, *Freaky Florida*, and *Creepy Florida*, talks about how he and his wife went on a road trip. In each town they crossed, they met interesting people and found new stories and versions that weren't online. Often, he's had someone whispering and waving him over to share the paranormal side of a place (Discover more about this on the *Drinking with Authors* podcast I co-hosted). It's a chance for you, as the author, to go on an adventure and build a unique connection to potential future readers!

FINAL THOUGHTS

If you are still having research headaches, take a break—or change focus! Sometimes you just need to stop researching and start writing to know what you need. Not every author and story needs research to start, and each genre has different reader expectations. Accuracy and the amount of history can shift hard between fantasy, historical fiction, and romance. Not all research involves historical items. At times you may be simply looking for locations for story plot points to fit the character's needs.

Just remember not to fall into the rabbit-hole, don't feel obligated to use all that you found, and be comfortable switching gears between research, writing, and revision. We don't always get everything in order before we start telling the story. Writing is a guessing game! Instead, leave yourself notes and keep your momentum with your work and writing efforts. Don't ever let research be a reason to procrastinate. Research should bring tools to the table to shape your story, characters, and the world you've built for them. When you're lost and need motivation, research should help you keep moving.

WRITING PROMPTS BASED ON RESEARCH

If you have attended any of my workshops, you know that I could base an entire session on how real life is stranger than fiction. Think of this as a fun writing prompt based on an obscure fact. I often split it up in the same manner as the research sections you saw earlier. There are some favorite facts and articles that I hand out, and then I ask the room of writers to write something inspired by what they have learned. The goal is not to recreate what is written there, but to use it to prevent writer's block, provide a means of thinking outside of the box, and be more confident in your own imagination, especially because real life can cook up something wilder. I am a firm believer in "Fact Inspiring Fiction." To give you some idea of this, here are some of the topics I often include:

PEOPLE

- Discovery of Zana: *the woman found in the wilds believed to be a Neanderthal!*
- Jack Churchill aka "Mad Jack": *World War II soldier who went to battle with claymore, longbow, and bagpipes!*
- Caterina Sforza: *lifted her skirt and flashed her enemies!*
- Grace O'Malley: *Irish pirate queen who sailed as far as Florida!*
- Adrian Paul Ghislain Carton de Wiart: *the unkillable World War II soldier!*
- Khutulun: *Mongolian Princess who wrestled men and won a giant herd of horses!*

EVENT

- New England Vampire Panic: *inspired Bram Stoker's Dracula!*
- Black Hawk War: *a terrible turning point in Native American history.*
- Blind Man to Walk Across World's Largest Salt Desert Guided Only by Audio GPS: *Enough said!*
- Mysterious Sealed Sarcophagus Found in Egypt: *These are always fun!*
- Bengal Famine of 1770-1772: *Firsthand accounts of this!*
- Pope Francis Credited with Performing "Miracle" as St. Gennaro's Blood Liquifies: *Wait, what?*

ANIMALS

- Suriname Toad: *lays its eggs inside the skin of its back!*
- Spook Fish: *has a transparent skull so it can look up*

- Lyrebird: *an amazing mimicker who has amazing feathers!*
- Hippopotamus: *They sweat blood. No joke!*
- Tasselled Wobbegong: *Not a joke—this is a real animal name and they are neat!*

- PLACES

  - The Underground Coal Fire That's Been Burning for 53 Years: *it glows at night still!*
  - Bones of 30,000 Plague Victims Decorate This Church: *it's called an ossuary!*

- GERLACH, NEVADA Fly Geyser: *he was digging a well—ended up with this!*

  o Lake Titicaca, South America: *highest elevated lake with cool low-oxygen creatures!*
  o Roanoke Colony: *no one knows where they went!*
  o The Bloody Pit: *dark U.S. railway history. Scary stuff!*

WHAT DO I DO WITH THE EXTRA RESEARCH?

What? You have excess information? Don't feel frustrated. It's normal for any writer or artist to have leftover materials and scraps. You've used all the parts you needed, but it's up to you as the writer to store the unused research for later, recycle it for the next project, create leads for readers and your newsletters, write short stories and make a companion or collection, or flaunt what you discovered.

In a later tome, you'll find that maintaining a newsletter is still the best way to drive sales, get feedback, increase book reviews, and so much more. Storing your leftover research for a rainy day can be helpful even as far ahead as the marketing and follow-up stage long after you have published the book. Never think the work you do at this stage (and don't use) doesn't have value elsewhere in your career as an author!

Did you know that the oracles were indeed real? I know this because...

I am terrible. You see, I take great pride in the depth of research I am willing to dive into, finding new levels as I descend! Below are some of the articles I have written for SciFiFantasyNetwork.com. They can still be found there if you want to share and/or reference them in order to inspire your own research!

Happy Reading & Writing!

THE ORACLE: MYTH OR REAL?

BY VALERIE WILLIS

Oracles have been some of the most mesmerizing characters in roleplaying games like *Dungeons & Dragons*, in books who foretell events within Fantasy and Science Fiction work like *The Last Oracle* by James Rollins, and even in the movie 300 where she warns of the fall of Sparta. At the core of it all, many will say the traditions of the oracle were part of Greek and Roman mythology. Visitors to Delphi, Greece are honored to visit the physical location where long ago The Oracle of Delphi sat upon the Sibyl Stone to give her predictions. Was she real or myth? While writing my novel, *The Oracle*, book three of The Cedric Series, I stumbled upon some amazing discoveries!

The word *oracle* is a late 14th century term, which makes its creation almost a thousand years late after the fall of the last known oracle (2,6). The term as we know it today implies a medium or messenger from god or fortune teller. Chasing the origins of the word to Old French finds a *temple or house prayer*, discovers the Latin *oraculum*, meaning *divine announcement*, and ends with the root of a long forgotten out-of-date language (Proto Indo-European perhaps). Here we uncover the foundation, *orare*, though still found in the Spanish language, which is defined as *to plead or beg*. Old or Archaic Latin, a foundation on which Latin and Romance languages were built, has vocal usage which predates its earliest known written forms dating in the seventh century BC on a belt buckle in rarely seen archaic writing (3). As for its connection to Oracles is unsure and simply has been translated as *"pray"* based on Latin proverbs that use this word.

This leads me to reveal the correct title during the age in which they existed—Ancient Greeks never called them oracles. Instead, the proper word would be *sibyl*. If we venture back into the word itself, the ancient Dorian (Yes, older than Archaic Latin that dates back to 75 BCE, Dorian dates back to 1,200 BCE) word *siobolla* meaning *divine wish* was adapted to *sibylla* in ancient Greek as the official term for *a woman possessed by powers of prophecy* (7). Ah, so now we are getting to the proper root of the matter. Oracle is a newer term, far from the proper title given to them during the time they lived.

IN THE BEGINNING...

The Oracle of Delphi is one of the more well-known oracles—a shrine to her dates as far back as 1400 BC. This fact is rather confusing since Greek mythology was first introduced orally during the "Age of Heroes" during the 11th century BC during the Bronze Age (4). A three-hundred-year gap stands between oracles and Greek mythology! During that time, they established a stronghold on Mt. Parnassus and began building alliances with local tribes. By the time they incorporated a belief system, changing their alliance from Gaea to Apollo, they had a shrine and devoted followers, including an established system for successors. We can only ponder why she wasn't deemed a goddess herself and wonder how the oracle in Delphi is devoted to Apollo. Wouldn't that mean Apollo predates his own mythos? Honestly, it puts his creation in Delphi at the same time he is created in Celtic mythology, but this obscure fact on Apollo will have to be saved for a later article!

DELPHI, GREECE

This location was first settled by small tribes in the Bronze Age, between 14-11th BC at around the same time the language which became the core language for conquerors of this part of the world. If you feel like this name feels familiar, note that this is one of the pivotal locations for the Olympics since the 20th Century, and before that, the Pythian Games. The location became subject to Roman rule in 191 BC (5), and it was here that the location was targeted for ransacking of treasuries and the scrutiny of Christian practices. Visiting the area today, you can see Mt. Parnassus and remnants of the temples on its plateau. The two significant locations here are the Sibyl Stone and Treasury of Apollo. At one point, Delphi was the center of the world for many ancient people, and at its core was the oracle or sibyl. By the 8th century BC, the oracle was internationally known, the most famous of oracles being Pythia (or at least best documented!).

Vapors would seep out of the earth and springs, chemicals inducing a hallucinogenic state and even ecstasy. The fumes were cold, boiling out of the Castalian Springs at the oracle's feet, beneath the tripod stool on which she sang, mumbled, and spoke her prophecies. It was sealed, or blocked off, after the temple fell apart during the last Roman raid. This is the speculated reason why many believe the oracle finally lost her hold on the world when the fumes lost their potency. Volcanic activities are not uncommon deep under the ground in this area—Mt. Vesuvius sits just across the Ionian Sea notorious for wiping out Pompeii and Herculaneum. Regardless, modern geologists have confirmed intoxicating fumes seeping up through the limestone and springs in the area.

THE FIRST ORACLE & THE SIBYL STONE

The stone is named in compliments of the first oracle, referred to as the Sibyl. Her real name was Herophile (6) though she is associated with several others. It was here in the beginning when the oracle was originally a speaker on behalf of Gaia herself. Herophile, the great prophetess who lived on the plateau of Mt. Parnassus, earned herself quite the reputation for her accuracy. She stood upon a chunk of stone where she would dictate her predictions, and later the sacred stone would be rightfully named the Sibyl Stone. Sadly, most of the books recording the many predictions were destroyed in fires. Many of them had been kept in Rome, but the fires in 84 BC and 69 AD would later devour what would have been left behind by the first oracle Herophile.

Despite it, there are some written pieces within the Sibylline Collection (8) which have a wonderful translated (and downloadable!) digital file. Herophile was a priestess of Gaia; who knows if she saw her home would turn into a landscape of temples and treasuries? Her famous abilities shocked the world countless times and even now, many speculate her words are randomly placed within the pages of the religious books which have withstood time, such as the Torah and Bible (8). These temples throughout Greek and Italy depict Apollo and his sister Artemis battling giants and monsters alike. One can't help but wonder if Herophile was Artemis herself. Mind you, Artemis predates Christianity and written Greek mythology.

GREEK & ROMAN INFLUENCES

During the Dark Ages and into Ancient Greece (12th century BC to 1st century BC), an alliance of tribes in Greece tasked themselves with defending the oracles in Delphi. The oracles shifted their own devotion from Gaia to Apollo to appeal to their protectors at this stage. Their influence was so great, they were depicted on Greek money early on in their ascension. Many kings and rulers travelled far and wide to see the oracle on the Sibyl Stone and later within the Temple of Apollo. Perhaps her advice allowed the tribes to stay hidden or avoid complete destruction by the unfolding turmoil.

Herophile and her successors were said to have written nine books, and a sibyl brought them to the Roman King Tarquinius. She demanded three hundred pieces of gold for them. When denied because the Romans didn't know what the books were, she threw three into the fire. Later, she approached again with the other six tomes, demanding the same price. This time the king humored her, looking over the words, astonished by the predictions. Thus began Rome's relationship with the oracle and the rise of a new wave of honoring Delphi. Unfortunately, those six books and those commissioned after the initial buy were later lost in fires. Regardless, the oracle once again proved she was fully capable of securing her own future with her own ability. The Oracle of Delphi represents an epitome of feminine power in a time where there is little evidence of female agency.

DOWNFALL OF THE ORACLE

The biggest discrepancy surrounds the time that the oracle faded from the world. One fact remains consistent: the sibyls were wiped out by Julian the Apostate, the Christian emperor who flipped back to paganism and turned to them for aid. Not just one, but several sibyls refused to aid him or provide one prophecy to him. In the translated Sibylline Collection, Book 12, line 316 predicts the coming of Julian and his destruction of many men. Perhaps this prior prophecy is why the oracles of his time refused to aid him (8). Outraged, Julian funded a campaign to wipe out all known sybils and their temples. The reign of the oracle fell, the last shrine emptied in 390 AD by the order of the Christian Emperor Theodosis (6) when the shrine was leveled.

The sibyls were an order of soothsayers who shook the world, spanning the Bronze Age, the Dark Ages, from Ancient times through the Age of Antiquity. Their followers came from a mixture of backgrounds from paganist Sabine tribes and Persian royalty to Christian Emperors. The Oracle of Delphi should be seen as an umbrella term for the nameless faces who foretold and forewarned the world of what was to come. If you wish to discover more, I highly encourage you to check out Sacred Texts and download the translated Sibylline books for yourself. The information provided in this article is a collaboration of many sources from history, myth, translations, and even the etymology of the words involved.

REFERENCES

1. http://gadling.com/2010/09/21/the-death-of-paganism-how-the-roman-empire-converted-to-christi/
2. http://www.etymonline.com/index.php?term=oracle
3. http://linguistics.byu.edu/classes/Ling450ch/reports/latin.html
4. http://ancient-greece.org/history/bronze-age.html
5. http://ancient-greece.org/history/delphi.html
6. http://www.crystalinks.com/delphi.html
7. http://www.etymonline.com/index.php?term=sibyl
8. http://www.sacred-texts.com/cla/sib/
9. http://www.biblicalarchaeology.org/daily/ancient-cultures/daily-life-and-practice/the-oracle-of-delphi%E2%80%94was-she-really-stoned/
10. http://www.coastal.edu/intranet/ashes2art/delphi2/misc-essays/oracle_of_delphi.html

VALERIE WILLIS

CELTIC APOLLO VERSUS GREEK APOLLO

BY VALERIE WILLIS

That's right—there are several versions of the God Apollo, but most come down to either Celtic or Greek versions. Granted, Celtic and Greek mythology developed in similar manners starting in the Bronze Age as spoken legends and history shared for centuries. The question here is: why only Celtic and Greek? Who is the real Apollo?

WHAT WE NEED TO KEEP IN MIND

Information is added and deleted from resource-to-resource and not knowing when that version was written or even first spoken, myth becomes a melting pot of variants. They contort in strange directions as they collide with other cultures and religions. In those early centuries, the Celts and Greeks had no interest in one another, let alone if they had knowledge of one another's existence. Eventually, a chain of events would drive the Celts to seek land to conquer toward the Mediterranean where they began to clash with one another. Due to this history, most of the accounts involving Celtic mythology and early events are written by their enemies, the Romans.

Greeks developed a written language and many of the temples throughout the land were tasked as keepers of written lore, legends, prophecies, and mythology. However, the Celts, viewed written history and mythology as an insult to their ancestor's oral practices. The individuals who devoted all their stories to memory were known as Druids. Due to this cultural bias, most of the original variants of the Celtic Mythos depend on very limited archaeological finds, written accounts from Romans after they had invaded Europe, or sadly, oral practices that had fallen apart and were revived since the days they had ruled supreme.

CELTIC APOLLO

The earliest written accounts involving the Celts are from the late sixth century BC. Hecateus of Miletus mentions a "City of Celts" called Narbonne, a port city in Southern France that gave the Celts access to the Greeks (and came under Roman rule by 118 BC). As stated before, the information we have about Celtic traditions, religion, and culture (prior to their defeat by the Romans) is written mostly by one Roman General: Julius Caesar. According to archaeological traces, even 1,400 years before the common era, there were no signs of written language. Still, Julius Caesar found it rather interesting they had gods resembling those the Romans had adopted from Greek mythology such as Ares, Hermes, and even Minerva. He even witnessed some of the written language they used in 58 BC which borrowed Greek lettering.

Regardless, we want to focus on Apollo. He noted simply that, in a similar fashion to the Romans, they prayed to Apollo—a god who warded against illness. The problem escalates from here because the Celts had a very detailed and large pool of gods. Part of the Roman campaign was to help convert their newly conquered citizens by giving their existing gods Roman labels, grouping them as if they were all the same single god of war, Mars or Ares, or merging multiples gods of commerce into one, Mercury! In turn, history has a ginormous list of Celtic gods with the name Apollo attached. Weeding through this list exposes some intriguing, crossed wires when you start comparing several resources side-by-side. During the Gallic Wars, the Celtic Apollo was indeed a totem for health. Despite it all, Romans were surprised to see the Celts had already adopted the namesake Apollo within their multitude of gods, yet it was clear the Greeks had very little involvement in the matter.

CELTIC APOLLO VERSUS GREEK APOLLO

The latest trend in the last thousand years leading up to the Common Era focused on the fact Apollo was immune to disease and the people's desire for the same immunity in the age of war and conquerors. Apollo is often associated with the sun, but the further you dig into the past, the larger the gap becomes with this connection. In fact, at some point misinformation developed of Belenus, a man and god of the sun in Gallic history, so this information is far too fresh, too close to the Common Era variants of Apollo worshipped and recorded in the last decades of the BC era.

The earliest Celtic Apollo can easily be seen as *Apollo Amarcolitanus*. His name implies he is the *Apollo of the distant gaze*, a phrase found on the continent where the Celts began. I cannot, nor has anyone else, explained how a Greek god was adopted by Druids who found him worthy to add to their complex oral tradition. Nor can we explain why none of the cultures and people between the Greek and Celtic continents, even according to Julius Caesar's own records in 58 BC, had heard of Apollo. Thus, the allure and magic of the Celtic mythology thrives.

GREEK APOLLO

Strange as it may seem, Greek mythology and early culture was passed on for centuries by oral traditions long before it finally developed into a written archaic Latin format. It's as if the cake ingredients for both cultures started the same, but how they were baked and presented to the world evolved in drastically different ways. Written accounts of Apollo can be found in the *Sibylline Texts*, but note you will not find "Apollo" written in its pages. Instead, a different and peculiar namesake is written here: *Patara*. Older Greek mythology involving the god associates him with wolves, not the sun, and even labels him at some point as the *King of Arcadia*.

Amazing to consider, but the sibyls, or oracles, invested in Apollo. Not only had they abandoned the original deity they were devoted to, Gaea or Gaia, but they used Apollo as a spearhead of interest from the local Greek tribes to help develop the Lycian Union as an impromptu bodyguard system for themselves. At this point, Apollo stood for protection and strength, which in turn explains why the Lycian League named their city Patara, keeping the early drafts of their constitution within a temple devoted to Apollo himself. If we look to Patara's beginnings, we refer to the time between the 8th and 12th century BC, the end of the Bronze Age.

Sybils spoke of their existence and devotion to Patara ceasing, and even cover the fall of the *din of Pataras*, but unlike so many kings, gods, and entities within those pages, never do they discuss the death of Patara or Apollo. In fact, Phoebus, who can also be seen as Artemis, Apollo's twin sister, was seen in the same light by the Celts as a false god or *hag* who would mislead men, despite her prowess and intelligence. Unlike the Celts, the Greeks had the oracles and other entities who wrote mythology and history down. Even this, though, can be just as mixed up and confusing as most of the instances found under Celtic mythology. Other resources state that Apollo rested in Patara for the winter or that it was his birthplace. Perhaps, if there was some legendary man during this influential time in Greece, he carried this name and lived as he were the god Apollo himself.

Greek Apollo has outlived his Celtic counterpart in popularity, but he also is one who is well documented with historical events that match many of his earlier tales. The stories involving Boreas of the Lykaon, one of the tribes who started the Lycian League, have historical roots. As the oracles even state, Nyctimus did indeed dissolve the throne after Boreas was slain. Many of the myths and legends state it was Apollo who killed him for all the sins he committed. Others dictate Zeus cursed Boreas and his men to live their lives as dog-headed men, which later inspired werewolf culture and lycanthropes.

> *O Lycians, Lycians, there shall come a wolf*
> *To lick thy blood, when Sannians shall come*
> *With city-wasting Ares and the Carpians*
> *Shall draw near with Ausonians to fight.*
> **190** *And then by his own shameless recklessness*
> *The bastard son shall put the king to death,*
> *And he himself for his impiety.*
>
> —Sibylline Sacred Texts

My Conclusion on the Matter

Here is where I leave you with my own quirky flair. Mind you, I am a fantasy romance author by trade who has a geeky talent for research via the books and internet articles I get my greedy fingers on. This was the sort of material I loved coming across when developing my character Romasanta in The Cedric Series.

Here it is... what are the chances the oracles sent warriors and believers of Apollo out on a pilgrimage? And by some obscure chain of events, one found himself in a new place where he brought the knowledge of Greek living into a still rather barbaric society who had a deity system so much like the one back home? Perhaps the Celtic Apollo carried a faraway gaze, one in which he longed for his original Greek home.

References

1. *The Encyclopedia of Celtic Mythology and Folklore* by Patricia Monaghan
2. Wikipedia on Narboone: https://en.wikipedia.org/wiki/Narbonne
3. *Sibylline Oracle Text*: http://www.sacred-texts.com/cla/sib/
4. Julius Caesar's Work: http://www.sacred-texts.com/cla/jcsr/index.htm
5. *The Dictionary of Mythology* by J.A.Coleman
6. *The Ultimate Encyclopedia of Mythology* by Arthur Cotterell & Rachel Storm
7. *The Encyclopedia of Ancient Myths and Culture* by Quantum Books
8. Lycia Government: http://www.lycianturkey.com/lycian_government.htm
9. Patara Findings of Lycian League: http://www.lycianturkey.com/lycia-american-constitution.htm

THE MOTHER OF DRAGONS IS NOT DAENERYS

BY VALERIE WILLIS

Game of Thrones has renewed our love for dragons. When the title "Mother of Dragons" is whispered among GOT fans, they are talking about Khaleesi Daenerys Targaryen. The real owner of this title is Delphyne, though there are inspirations taken from this figure from Greek mythology. They look very different from one another with Delphyne described as a massive half-woman, half-dragon entity. Her story crosses the path of more familiar entities such as Zeus, Apollo, and even the oracles. At some point in her tale, she fell in love with the King of Monsters and later gave birth to all monsters and dragons of the world. There is a tragic romance about the original mother of dragons, much like our beloved Khaleesi, but her story faded from modern listings of Greek mythology. Granted, what follows is a combination of resources from all over and my own speculations on her story.

Delphyne and Delphinus were words developed during the late Roman language timeframe, but the root word delphys for womb goes back to Ancient Greek. Even the alternate version, Delphine, dates to the 14th century meaning a woman from Delphi, but sources older than this point become mangled or disappear altogether. Much of the ancient context and uses for this root word is overlaid with the references of dolphins and their current Latin genus name of delphinidae making research a disaster at best.

Both Delphyne and her lover Typhon were described as half-human on the top with bottom half of a dragon or serpent. Delphyne has also been labeled as drakaina, a feminine form of drakon, which later gave birth to the modern term of dragon. In later artwork, the human half was replaced with a more dragon-like creature and look with fangs, wings, and an animalistic head. There are examples of this shift with artwork featuring Apollo versus Typhon, sometimes labelled Python, on vases, statues, and even artwork in the centuries long after the Romans fell.

Delphyne is consistently marked as the Mother of Dragons in several places, but unlike Typhon, she is not found on pottery or in artwork. It's a peculiar absence that shows the limitations of online information. Despite it all, there is a chain of events mentioned in a wide variety of areas. Stories of other titans and gods in translated books like Argonautica can be pieced together to give some insight to Delphyne's story. Here are my gathered snippets put into a more complete telling of who the mother of dragons was, and her journey in short.

The intriguing part is how several sources indicate Delphyne is a daughter of Gaea, the mother of all the major titans, yet she is not listed among her siblings. You will not find her next to any of her sisters or brothers in the family trees and flow charts tracking the breakdown of the godly family which make up the foundation of Greek mythology. Instead, you get snippets here and there of her name being mentioned, dropped in obscure places stretching between Greek and Roman tales. For example, the Hymn of Phoebe, her maternal sister, sings of her son Apollo's feat:

> *"...once beneath the rocky ridge of Parnassus he slew with his bow the monster Delphyne..."*
> —*Argonautica*, book 2, translated by R. C. Seaton

Delphyne was born from Gaea, mother of earth, to serve as the womb for all the creatures of the world. From lore on Gaea, the mother of all titans, it becomes clear she and her son Kronus grew jealous of the creation of mankind. Delphyne was first gifted to Kronus, perhaps a means of torturing mankind—no one will ever know. At this point, Kronus was not satisfied with his mother's gift, or decided it would be better to give her to his son Zeus.

At this point, we are on a more familiar name and entity, the god who led the Olympians and was famous for his lightning. Zeus took care of her at this point as a sort of pet, but I believe she may have inspired the later tales of the Gorgons such as the famous Medusa.

At some point, Zeus enraged his grandmother Gaea, and before he knew it, she had sculpted a creature from the Earth itself to come for him:

> *"The one seemed to be a monstrous son of baleful Typhoeus or of Earth herself, such as she brought forth aforetime, in her wrath against Zeus..."*
> —*Argonautica*, book 2, translated by R. C. Seaton

The tale goes on as to how Typhon came and stole the sinews of Zeus and took them to Mt. Parnassus in hope of gaining or perhaps stealing his power. It was Delphyne who came to Zeus' rescue, battling Typhon and reclaiming Zeus' sinews. She protected the god until he recovered. It is here that things fade or jump around. What can be assumed is she came under fire from Gaea for intervening, which never bodes well for anyone in the other stories involving her, so Zeus gave Delphyne away. It seems sad, to think she was handed off again to Zeus' Aunt Phoebe, though she gave Delphyne her final home.

Being the Titaness who established the sibyls, or oracles, she gave Delphyne the task of being the protector of the Oracle on Mt. Parnassus. There seems to be some interesting overlap when you compare different stories and snippets mentioning Delphyne. At this point, some imply she was chained to the mountain, cared for by the nymphs who name the great ancient city Delphi in her honor. Even more intriguing is the implication that Typhon joined her in her task, and Mt. Parnassus became the origin point in which all monsters and dragons came into the world. Hence the official titles *Mother of Dragons* and *Father of Monsters* were established.

Soon Phoebe's son Apollo came to Mt. Parnassus, and it is here that we find a weird mixture. Only one mentions that it is Delphyne he slays. Artwork and several other sources show it was Typhon, or Python, whom he kills. Again, this flips from a half-man version on older vases to a full-fledged dragon in later paintings. Oddly enough, the oracles here on the mountain worshipped Apollo at this point. This seems accurate when you consider that the mountain, the sibyls, and even the guardian dragons were all owned by his mother Phoebe, depending on which snippet you chase to the one sliver of information left behind.

It is never clear as to why Apollo came to the mountain, other than to seek counsel of the oracle. Nor does it make sense why he needed to fight his way to a temple devoted to him (and owned, founded even, by his mother who adored him) from how the mythology unfolds. Regardless, Apollo came and brought an end to the *Mother of Dragons* or at least killed her lover. Perhaps she is still on Mt. Parnassus, alone and forgotten. It's a tragic ending to the less glamorous life she had endured—a lot of similarities to Khaleesi's own tragic start. The question is, will the King of Arcadia and sigil of the wolf, Apollo, make his debut in *Game of Thrones* and slay the *Mother of Dragons* like the Greek influence suggests?

REFERENCES

1. *The Dictionary of Mythology* by J.A.Coleman
2. *Giants, Monsters, & Dragons* by Carol Rose
3. Etymology of Delphine–https://en.wiktionary.org/wiki/Delphine
4. *Argonautica* Book 2, translated by RC Seaton–http://www.theoi.com/Text/ApolloniusRhodius2.html
5. Python–http://www.theoi.com/Ther/Drakaina-Python.html
6. *Encyclopedia of Beasts and Monsters in Myth, Legend, & Folklore* by Theresa Bane; https://books.google.com/books?id=DvYWDAAAQBAJ&pg=PA99&lpg=PA99&dq=Greek+mythology+Delphyne&source=bl&ots=kTRWb9I1z3&sig=m16LqlLdIlbAHtEZTACXigJ8Fwg&hl=en&sa=X&ved=0ahUKEwielJeEzorWAhWBdyYKHVoBDEI4ChDoAQgnMAA#v=onepage&q=Greek%20mythology%20Delphyne&f=false
7. GOT Wiki: Daenerys Targaryen–http://gameofthrones.wikia.com/wiki/Daenerys_Targaryen
8. Echidna – Delphyne Wiki–https://en.wikipedia.org/wiki/Echidna_(mythology)#Delphyne
9. Drakaina – Delphyne Greek–https://en.wikipedia.org/wiki/Drakaina_(mythology)
10. Typhon–https://en.wikipedia.org/wiki/Typhon
11. Delphyne–https://en.wikipedia.org/wiki/Delphyne
12. Drakones–http://www.theoi.com/Ther/DrakonesTroiades.html
13. Titanides–http://www.theoi.com/Titan/Titanides.html
14. Nymphai Korykai–http://www.theoi.com/Nymphe/NymphaiKorykiai.html

VALERIE WILLIS

EVOLUTION OF VAMPIRES

BY VALERIE WILLIS

Vampires. We see them on television, in books, featured in artwork, and during Halloween, we love to dress up like them. Where does it all come from? What defines the vampire we see today versus the one our ancestors whispered about during those dark nights by the fire? There may not be any clear answer to this, no straight path to follow, but you will find many examples all over the world, including Hindu, Romanian, Greek, Japanese, and even Native American lore. This mythology is deeper than Bram Stoker's *Dracula* and older than Vlad the Impaler. Let's take it back to those first inklings and work our way to the familiar veins, shall we? Much of this research is part of a ten+ year project for my dark fantasy paranormal romance, The Cedric Series, so let's take a swim together. This is a multi-part series, be sure to check back for the next installments often.

WHAT DEFINES A VAMPIRE

Before we go down the black hole of historical accounts, let's take a moment to discuss what makes a thing a vampire? In today's world, it defaults to drinking blood and inability to be in the sunlight, but as we crawl farther back, this becomes less apparent. Instead, many of the early versions of "vampires" or similar creatures straddle both the walking dead or witches featuring various abilities. Shapeshifting, flying, melting into shadows, possession, and other elements have been included long before the more practical blood drinkers. Many of these early editions served as people-eaters and life-suckers rather than the common blood eating sort we know and love.

> *We will consider anything that feeds on humans by blood or soul a vampire.*

Demons and creatures who eat people are a whole different ball game, which includes the common reference to *Lilith or Lilitu* of Jewish and Assyrian mythology as well as the Babylonian demi-goddess *Lamashtu or Lamassu*. That's right—I just said they don't count as vampires, so hold on to your hats folks; you're in for a long ride. Granted, some of the historical accounts feature cannibalistic entities, but they play a huge part in modern fiction's vampire evolution.

THE MEANING BEHIND THE WORD *VAMPIRE*

Though I may be using vampire as a generic umbrella term, you should be aware this is a rather new word or label for our blood and soul-sucking favorites. This version of the word, *vampire*, was first widely noted in a 1734 French tome about current burial practices. Belief in vampires and the art of digging them up to stake or burn their hearts spread like wildfire throughout the 1700 and 1800's. This may be in part to the conditions which brought people to a death-like sleep, and with no medical science to safely know the difference, being buried alive was common (Check out more on this topic on the podcast <u>Lore, episode 72, "A Grave Mistake"</u>).

Parts of the word may come from a Slavic word for *witch*, *upyr*, or even Russian words such as *upir (witch)* or *netopyr*, meaning bat. *Upir* appears in an 11th century tome but had become *vampir* by the Renaissance in the 15th century (Vlad the Impaler's reputation set it in motion). Occasionally, the word would be misspelled, giving birth to the 1700-1800's variant of *vampyre*. Looking to the Ancient Greek word *vapi*, one must wonder if it joined, distorted, and mingled in the cultures to the North and West for the final edition of *vampir or vampire*. Broken apart, and applied to Greek and Latin, *vapi* means *will drink or to drink*, with *upir* or *pir* meaning *witch* (the *drinking witch* or perhaps the *Witch who will drink?*). The oldest written version of any of these

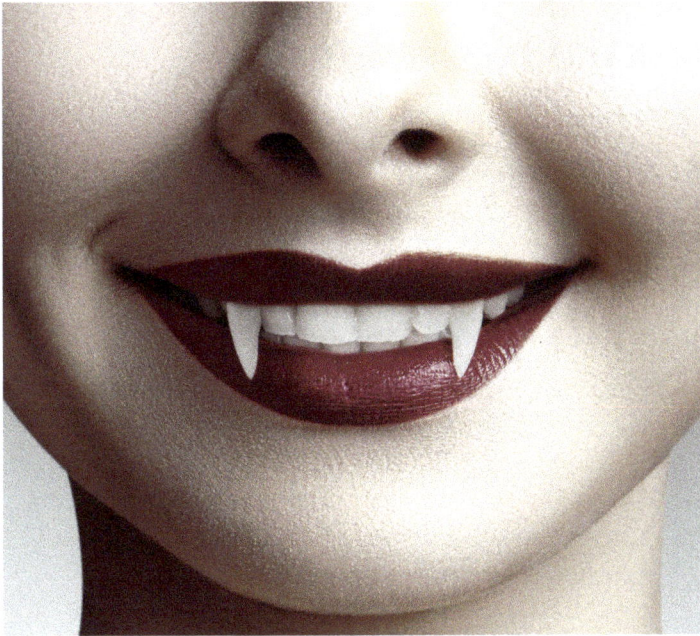

CE in a story about *Upir Lichyj* or *wicked vampire* referring to a Slavic Priest.

Before this, we had other terms—the Romanian term *strigoi*, meaning *hag or evil spirit*, was common among traveling merchants. Derived from a root of the Romanian verb *striga, to scream*, this later gave birth to a variant *strix*, meaning *screech owl* (a bird of ill omen that fed on human flesh and blood in Greek mythology). Later, this word described a type of *witch*. In some places, the witch, the werewolf, and the vampire were all the same. Many tales of the *varga mor* tell of a soul-sucking, or man-eating, witch who could turn into a wolf.

The word *moroi* closely follows *strigoi* in the old Romanian folklore. It derives from the Romanian word *mora*, meaning *nightmare*. Another connection is the Russian *kikimora*, but much of their lore wasn't written down. In general, *kikimora* were considered offspring of a werewolf or vampire, and like the *strigoi*, variants of dead and alive versions are scattered between the verbal and written tales of the Middle Ages. I would like to note—tales of werewolves date well-before vampire lore and have far more names and accounts noted. Hence, in The Cedric Series why book two, *Romasanta: Father of Werewolves* unfolds as it does, implying that werewolves created vampires.

OLDEST WRITTEN ACCOUNTS OF A VAMPIRE

Not every culture and religion focused on recording or writing down its tales, mythology, beliefs and lifestyle. A great example of this would be the Celtic people who believed in having Druids pass along their stories and religion via oral tradition or verbal storytelling. Think of a Druid as some kind of bard, since they would sing songs and tell legends of old. Regardless, my aim is to start this journey on what had factual dates or roundabout starting points. Let's start on familiar ground, then we will make our way to a time before.

THE BIBLE & NEW TESTAMENT

> *"I saw the woman, drunk with the blood of the saints and with the blood of the martyrs of Jesus. And when I saw her, I marveled with great amazement."*
>
> *Revelations 17:6*

The Bible is smattered with messages which can be taken literally or symbolically. In some instances, it seems clear the message is powerful men taking from the poor or condemning the ill. Other times, you wonder if there is some link to the belief of vampires. In short, the Old Testament makes it very clear we are not to drink the blood of others for fear of becoming something different, something cursed. Revelations 17:6 has one chilling moment, and one must wonder what sort of vampire had her fill, or will be doing so, in the Apocalypse to come. Granted, in a more symbolic manner, this is about taking in one's faith and letting it fill them to their core. Regardless, the Bible dates back about 2,700 years and isn't the oldest written account.

THE TORAH AND OLD TESTAMENT

> *"If any one of the house of Israel or of the strangers who sojourn among them eats any blood, I will set my face against that person who eats blood and will cut him off from among his people."*
>
> *Leviticus 17:10*

The Torah, or as some say, the Old Testament, predates the modern Bible, setting it about 3,300 years old. Leviticus pushes for man to be mindful of one fact: *blood is life.* Thus, the lesson is instilled one who drinks the blood of others will be cast out, or perhaps, no longer considered a man. It wasn't until the Talmud in 200 CE when the Jewish vampire began its roots as seducers known as *strigas, succubi,* and their lead seductress, Lilith. Teamed with the teachings from the Zohar and Kabbalah practices in the 2nd Century CE, blending demon, witch, vampires, and magic users became a widely known "fact" to those in the known world. Still, Leviticus holds true to blood-drinking mortals turned vampire.

THE SIBYLLINE ORACLES

> *"505 With supplications and unholy rites.*
> *Forsaking the Creator they were slaves*
> *To lewdness. Men possessing everything*
> *Bestow their gifts on things which cannot aid,*
> *As if they for my honors deemed these things*
> *510 All useful, with the smell of sacrifice*
> *Filling the feast, as if for their own dead.*
> *For they flesh and bones full of marrow burn*
> *Offering on altars, and they pour out blood*
> *To demons, and they kindle lights to me*
> *515 The giver of light, and as to a god*
> *That thirsts do mortals drunken pour out wine*
> *For nought to idols that can give no aid.*
> *I have no need of your burnt offerings,*
> *Nor your libations, nor polluted smoke,*
> *520 Nor blood most hateful. For in memory*
> *Of kings and tyrants they will do these things*
> *Unto dead demons, as to heavenly beings,*
> *Performing service godless and destructive.*
> *And godless they their images call gods,"*
>
> *Sybilline Book VIII*

Let's not forget the sibyls, or oracles, had their fair share in recording the idea these blood drinkers existed (See my article on the oracles above for more about their historical roots). The Sibylline books were written as far back as the 6th Century BC, making them roughly 5,000 years old. Between a fire in 83 BC and the Roman General Flavius Stilicho (365-408 CE), a large portion of the Sibylline texts were lost to the world. Still, what has survived contains remnants of the Bible and Torah, and a lot more to say about the drinking of blood.

Again, echoes of Leviticus can be found along with some chilling ideas of vampire worshipping and the judgment that comes from an immortal god. Book II, verse 115 of the Sibylline text says: "When he to judgment comes, disable not Thy mind with wine nor drink excessively. Eat not blood, and abstain from things offered to idols." It seems as if blood drinking is the same as making a pact with something, or meant for non-humans entirely, and here, the Sibyl warns to stay sober lest you fall prey.

Twenty-Five Tales of Baital

> "Madhusadan proceeded to make his incantations, despite terrible sights in the air, the cries of jackals, owls, crows, cats, asses, vultures, dogs, and lizards, and the wrath of innumerable invisible beings, such as messengers of Yama (Pluto), ghosts, devils, demons, imps, fiends, devas, succubi, and others. All the three lovers drawing blood from their own bodies, offered it to the goddess Chandi, repeating the following incantation, "Hail! supreme delusion! Hail! goddess of the universe! Hail! thou who fulfillest the desires of all. May I presume to offer thee the blood of my body; and wilt thou deign to accept it, and be propitious towards me!"
>
> *Vikram and the Vampire* by Sir Richard F. Burton

At the end of this list is a more obscure piece with an origin date unknown. *Baital Pachisi, or Twenty-five tales of Baital* was written in an ancient Hindu language known as *Sanskrit (the language of the gods)* which dates as far back as 600 BC. This is a vampire story nearly 1,000 years older than the Sibyl's own writings with a rewritten account in 1037 CE when the original scrolls were decaying. Later, Sir Richard F. Burton wrote an English adaptation, though loosely based on the original version, called *Vikram and the Vampire*. *Baital* was the name of a celestial spirit known as a *pishacha*, or for our convenience, *vampire*. According to legends, the *pishacha* fed on human energy or souls, hung upside down in trees, and much more.

Considering the snippets strewn across these ancient times, vampires were feared as soul suckers enticed by human blood. Humans also wanted their power, their immortality, even their blessing, and would drink blood to become something more.

Historical Accounts of Vampires

Fact often can be stranger, or more horrific, than fiction. What one creates in the imagination can be kept secret, but when actual blood is spilled, the world is forever stained, especially for the people affected. It's hard to make up a story when the monster leaves evidence of death and destruction in its wake. These bloodsucking and soul-shattering monsters had faces, names, and more harrowing, were made of flesh and bone like humans.

UPIR LICHY – 1047 CE

Written in a Slavic document using proto-Russian language, *upir lichy* refers to a priest of all people, meaning *wicked vampire*. This is during the time of Vladimir Jaroslav, Prince of Novgorod in Northwest Russia and a stickler for recording his encounters and things he faced. These were times of drastic change with Mongol attacks, Christianity growth and movement, the condemnation of Paganistic and old Slavic religions, and even later the Roman and Turk expansion. Turmoil and rage poured into Prince Jaroslav's country from all corners of the world. Converting his land and people to Christianity, he declared war on Paganism.

What followed I cannot say, having no luck finding a translated direct copy of this *Book of Prophets or Prophecies* matching the dates to confirm. The assumption here is that the wicked vampire priest was a Pagan one, or possibly one who straddled the two religions. Declared a heretic for holding onto his beliefs, he was perhaps seen as "barbaric" in the eyes of the Roman religion pressed on his peers. Either way, this soul-stealing vampire priest was labeled as such in the pages of history books.

In general, the *upir* was a sort of witch or sorcerer, who upon their death came back to life as a vampire. They were said to be punished, unable to rest in peace for their heresy against the Orthodox Church. Selling their souls to the devil, they gained powers and preyed upon the living, stealing souls and converting others. You can see a lot of tie-ins in opposing and converting religious beliefs. Fear was a factor for reorganizing and condemning those faithful to their former religion.

SIR GILLES DE RAIS – THE VAMPIRE OF BRITTANY – 1404-1440 CE

You may not recognize this name, but you should know he was famous for fighting and being a companion of Joan of Arc. In 1440, a large number of confessions hit a marshal in the accounts of kidnapped or missing children and the widespread belief that they were sacrificed to the devil. Unable to ignore this, Gilles was brought to trial. No one knows how many (mostly boys) fell victim to Gilles and his accomplices, but 140 victims were listed, ranging from poor unknowns to the sons of high-ranking families. A war hero of prestigious birth and rank became a monster after losing Joan and the war's end.

> *"How many children do you estimate that the Sire de Retz and his servants have killed?"*
>
> *"The reckoning is long. I, for my part, confess to having killed twelve with my own hand, by my master's orders, and I have brought him about sixty. I knew that things of the kind went on before I was admitted to the secret."*
>
> *The Book of Were-wolves* by Sabine Baring-Gould

Some say it was his grief and desire to prove there was no God driving him to such drastic and terrible deeds. His confessions

sound as if his devotion to God would forgive him for all and any sins he would desire to commit. Anything found in the Bible he would commit, from drinking blood as stated in Leviticus to sacrificing the youthful in the name of Satan and even raping and eating his victims. A few think he was innocent and this was a conspiracy to wipe away one of Joan's allies, but he confessed to his accusations. Within forty-eight hours, he was said to shift from belligerent to calm to crying out a sermon before he was hung at the gallows.

VLAD III OF WALLACHIA – DRACULA – 1439 CE

Vlad the Impaler is a story we all know. Vlad II sold his son as part of a peace treaty to the Turks. Upon earning a reputation, Vlad was granted leave to go home and that's when hell broke loose. Prior to this, his father joined the Order of the Dragon, dubbed the title *drac* meaning *dragon*. In Romanian, this word had another association and meaning: *devil*. Thus, Vlad earned titles as *son of the dragon/devil*. Whether he drank the blood of his enemies or was simply bloodthirsty is hard to say at this point. The bloodshed was the result of his position as the Prince of Wallachia. He immediately stopped paying homage to the Sultan, and invited any against this over for a dinner where stabbings and impaling made up the final course.

It is believed that his years imprisoned in the dungeon of Tokat Castle and time spent in battle made him no stranger to killing any who stood in his way. He took credit for impaling merchants and villagers all over Romania, especially those who made the mistake of ever doing business with his enemies in the past. Indeed, he used the rule of his namesake as the *devil.* As for where he was laid to rest, it's still a mystery historians chase. Regardless, he has been inspiration for a lot of vampire fiction including *Dracula* (novel), *Vampire Hunter D* (anime and short novel series), *The Historian* (novel), and countless Dracula movies, for better or worse.

COUNTESS ELIZABETH BATHORY – THE BLOOD COUNTESS – 1560-1614 CE

Not only was she said to drink the blood of countless young girls, but she bathed in the stuff. Though her family swept this "hobby of hers" under the rug for a long time, her thirst and ferocious desires eventually became too great. She preferred to surround herself with youth, most of her servant girls aged nine to fourteen. Many of the villagers lost their daughters to her stern and cruel practices. During the dead of winter, she had one girl punish another by tossing water on her in the courtyard until she froze to death. She was a cruel monster.

One fateful moment set Countess Bathory's obsession with blood into motion. A girl had been brushing her hair, and unfortunately, snagged or tugged too hard. The Countess slapped her, landing on the girl's ear, and hit with such force, she burst the poor thing's eardrum. Blood spurted across the Countess, but when she wiped it away, she noticed something—her skin was soft, youthful where the blood had been—thus birthing the bloodshed that inspired modern writers of vampire fiction. In January of 1611, she and her cohorts, or dealers, were put on trial for 80 counts of murder. Her punishment for her crimes? They bricked the Countess into her room and fed her through a slit in the wall for three years before she died in August 1614. She was stopped only when she turned her appetite to the daughters of the nobility.

FREDERICK RANSOM – WOODSTOCK VAMPIRE – 1817

Sometimes the title of *vampire* doesn't come from what bloodthirsty actions they took, but something out of one's control. Tuberculosis was spreading fast, even in Vermont. With symptoms such as coughing up blood, a pale and walking-dead appearance, and how it seemed to "suck the souls from those around them" (due to how contagious the disease could be in the right environment), panic ensued. Frederick died at the age of twenty. Immediately after, his brother fell horribly ill. Fearing Frederick was sucking the life from his brother and would soon come back from the grave for the remaining family, Frederick's father did the only thing he knew of: dug up his son's body.

> Telltale signs of vampirism would be blood around the mouth, a bloated corpse, a heart with blood still in it, and nails and hair appearing longer.
>
> Gareth Henderson from *The Vermont Standard*

Daniel Ransom, the younger brother, wrote in his memoir of the event, despite being three at the time. They exhumed his brother's body, cut out his heart, and burnt it in a blacksmith's fire. What no one realized is how fast this vampire accusation would spread decades later. Many of the accused were nothing more than victims of the pandemic of tuberculosis where medical science wasn't widespread enough to help cure the ill or even prevent the spread.

LENA MERCY BROWN – NEW ENGLAND VAMPIRE PANIC – 1892

Though early on our historical vampire inspirations came from ancient locales, America takes the belief to a new level. One well-documented case happened in Exeter, Rhode Island when the family of George and Mary Brown was riddled with consumption or tuberculosis. As one after another fell ill and died, neighbors and friends were convinced the Brown family was targeted by a vampire. At this point in history, they believed one of the family members was the creature and would have to be exhumed.

Desperate, George gave permission to do just that. On March 17th 1892, a large gathering came to watch as they exhumed all the bodies of his family while his last surviving member, his son Edwin, lay ill-stricken. Among these corpses was the mother who died first, followed by the eldest daughter Mary Olive who died in 1883, and lastly, the youngest, Mercy who died in 1891. One by one, villagers, a doctor, and a newspaper reporter witnessed to this drastic measure. It was Mercy's body that shocked them all. Unlike the others, her body had been kept in a freezer-like aboveground vault, thus her liver and heart still held blood. She had only been dead for two months and kept there since the ground in winter was too frozen to bury anyone.

Regardless, her heart was burnt, a tonic made of its ashes, mixed with water and given to Edwin in hopes of freeing him from the vampire's spell. He died two months later. The events in 1892 were so well reported in America that Bram Stoker, a stage manager from a theatre group from London, saved a copy of poor little Mercy's exhumation when he went home. Upon his death, a copy of the article was found tucked inside one of his journals.

"HIGH ALBANIA, CHAPTER IV" BY MARY EDITH DURHAM—1909

Mary Edith Durham first discovered tales of the *shtriga or striga* during her time with the Seltze tribe. She discovered very quickly that all the tribes she would encounter shared this same belief. The villagers told how the *striga* could be undetected in a village for years. These fiendish creatures were believed to be a sort of female vampire, blending in, feeding on the blood of children, enchanting grown folk, and making people shrivel up and die. Durham says the Kilmeni tribe had a sure way of catching one:

> *It is to keep the bones of the last pig you ate at carnival, and with these to make a cross on the door of the church upon Easter Sunday, when it is full of people. Then if the Shtriga be within, she cannot come out, save on the shoulders of the man that made the cross. She is seen, terrified, vainly trying to cross the threshold, and can be caught.*
>
> Mary Edith Durham

It was important to hunt the *striga* down, for she alone could heal her own victims. Mary was even told how one man's father had saved a child. A child was dead, white and cold, and his father dragged an old woman into the home. Drawing a pistol, he demanded she spit in the child's mouth to bring it back to life. When she relented, the child came back to life, and she was punished soon after. There are many more accounts she records in High Albania, and I encourage you to indulge in her fascination with the wave of strongly held superstitions in these villages she visited. Even at the turn of the 20th Century, the belief in this vampire was very real to a large, mixed community in Albania.

VAMPIRES WITHIN OLDER FICTION

We know of *Dracula*, but there were many other pieces written with vampires or vampire-like beings. Some insist they are female, others that they change, and many tie them to the grave. With illnesses like tuberculosis and nobility drinking the blood of their subjects, it wasn't hard to find inspiration. No one was safe from the powers of a vampire. They could haunt you like a ghost, steal your soul or life, and drink blood as if they were the devil himself. Thus, stories were told to capture the imagination.

VAMPYRISMUS BY BARON GERHARD VAN-SWIETEN – 1768

> *The magic of the deceased (Magia posthuma) was then in vogue in those areas. They called the dead, who were so vicious, vampires, and believed that they suck human blood.*
> *Vampyrismus* by Baron Gerhard van-Swieten—Rough Translation

Written in German, this was essentially a mockumentary designed to bring to light the rampage of labeling the deceased and diseased as a supernatural vampire. The Baron would never know that some folks took his piece very literally, despite his introduction declaring "these are fake notes written in German." He had defined them, identified them, spoke of what they could do and proper disposal of these creatures of ill-will. It was meant to be humorous, but in a time when panic and pandemics were putting entire families in the grave, the mind did wonder.

THE VAMPYRE: A TALE BY JOHN WILLIAM POLIDORI – 1819

> *"There was no colour upon her cheek, not even upon her lip; yet there was a stillness about her face that seemed almost as attaching as the life that once dwelt there:—upon her neck and breast was blood, and upon her throat were the marks of teeth having opened the vein:—to this the men pointed, crying, simultaneously struck with horror, "A Vampyre! a Vampyre!"*
> *The Vampyre: a Tale* by John William Polidori

This is a great example of a trend of spelling vampire as *vampyre* during the 1700-1800's. The introduction to this piece is amazing, and he discusses the fact consumption, tuberculosis, had much of the grounding in the research and belief of vampires in the time he wrote this piece. If you were looking for some great resources, this is a good fictional piece with some of the inspirations revealed upfront. He quotes work, such as *The Giaour,* along with people within this period and connects vampires to heresy. Remember, that's why *Upir Lichy* was convicted as a vampire in 1047 CE. Regardless, his writing brings this bloodsucking thirst and desire to life. In a few ways, there's this tinge of romanticism. I wonder if this piece influenced Bram Stoker's *Dracula.*

VIKRAM AND THE VAMPIRE BY SIR RICHARD F. BURTON – 1870

> *Scarcely, however, had the words passed the royal lips, when the Vampire slipped through the fingers like a worm, and uttering a loud shout of laughter, rose in the air with its legs uppermost, and as before suspended itself by its toes to another bough.*
>
> *Vikram and the Vampire* by Sir Richard F. Burton

A loosely based version of one of the oldest written lore, Burton describes quite the adventure, introducing the *baital* or vampire of the mischievous sorts. Here we have a blood and flesh-eating being in the form of a giant demonic bat. It hangs from a tree and can dissolve into mist. Later in the story, it possesses and hypnotizes people and shenanigans ensue. The vampire in these tales is a master of trickery and illusion. Not only does it change appearance, but the vampire can change the appearance of others. It seems the vampire in this story allows itself to be captured by Vikram, then grows curious and asks questions about his identity and past. Amused by the stubborn captor, the *baital* reminds Vikram to keep his manners and speak nicely to him, especially since Vikram will be strapping him to his back like a beggar's wallet by use of his waistcloth.

RUSSIAN FAIRY TALES BY RALSTON – 1872

> *Nor does their evil influence die with them, for after they have been laid in the earth, they assume their direst aspect, and as Vampires bent on blood, night after night, they go forth from their graves to destroy.*
>
> *Russian Fairy Tales* by Ralston

I love Russian fairy tales, and they have their share of vampire references. They also include numerous tales of wizards and witches, who are one and the same. That's right, when a witch or wizard dies and is buried, they come back as vampires! Granted they were said to have sold their souls to the devil, but it is an intriguing idea that someone who can cast spells and use magic gets this added bonus.

There was also belief that the devil would collect their souls to free their bodies for use by demons. In this

scenario, the vampire would still venture out to drink the blood of the living. It is also in these tales that the idea vampires must return to their coffins by the rooster's crow as in the story *The Coffin-Lid*. It is said people are more likely to run into a vampire at crossroads or the neighborhood of a cemetery and it's advised to not be in these places when night falls.

Another fun story within this collection is *The Two Corpses:* two vampires argue about who will get to eat a soldier returning home. The interesting part is one corpse comes from the graveyard while the other is inside a church. By the end of the story, the rooster crows and they fall dead. The soldier lives, praising the Lord for saving him from the *wizards*.

Carmilla by Joseph Sheridan Le Fanu – 1872

> *"Your mother warns you to beware of the assassin."* At the same time a light unexpectedly sprang up, and I saw Carmilla, standing, near the foot of my bed, in her white nightdress, bathed, from her chin to her feet, in one great stain of blood.
>
> *Carmilla* by Joseph Sheridan Le Fanu

If you feel like you know this one, yet not sure, it's because it has influenced many modern authors. One of my favorite references to *Carmilla* has to be from the anime movie and short novel series, *Vampire Hunter D* (Spirit of Carmilla scene: https://youtu.be/wmskV9CGTOM). In fact, it is implied D's father is Dracula and Carmilla is his stepmother, while his birth mother was human. Anyhow, in this piece, the main character finds himself caught in a strange situation. He begins to see a ghostly version of Carmilla at the foot of his bed and within the mansion. Upon investigation, the cast comes to agree she is a vampire, and they discover her coffin. The intriguing aspect here is the tie-in with Elizabeth Bathory—Carmilla bathes in blood, and her coffin is filled with the stuff.

BRAM STOKER'S *DRACULA* – 1897

> *He was lying on his belly on the floor licking up, like a dog, the blood which had fallen from my wounded wrist. He was easily secured, and, to my surprise, went with the attendants quite placidly, simply repeating over and over again: "The blood is the life! The blood is the life!"*
>
> *Dracula* by Bram Stoker

Taking in the literature and historical accounts of vampires, this novel continues to dazzle modern audiences. Bram Stoker did some research, some reading, and even saved clippings about the "New England Vampire" epidemic during his time touring with his theatre group in 1892. This work of fiction took a little bit from everywhere for one grand finale, the firework show everyone would remember. You can find references from various places such as the Bible, *Carmilla*, and many of the works we discussed. He romanticized the story and thanks to his experience as a stage manager, he was able to capture the audience where others had failed.

Today, readers still know Dracula, and many of will ask, "Bram Stoker's? Or Vlad the Impaler?" Stoker created a journaled account of one man's struggle to save the love of his life while confronting the supernatural in ways he never thought possible. Stoker suggests that vampires are nobility in their own right, but creatures deserving of pity at times. From this point, Bram Stoker was a driving force inspiring the present-day vampire and encouraging writers to dive deeper into stranger territory and leave the readers thirsting for more.

CONCLUSION

I like to think by the time the 1900's took hold, the belief in the real vampire faded away. This belief imprisoned our ancestors and entranced their descendants, but as medical science improved, fewer "dead" returned from the grave. Humans learned about tuberculosis, that germs can take out entire households, and the monsters were merely human, and humans could stop them. This vampire journey has gone far down the unbeaten path. Though there were Greek goddesses and Babylonian demi-gods, I wanted to take a journey less walked, reviewed, and reflected on.

Vampires are part of our culture, they always have been, but they aren't haunting and feeding off our families anymore. Instead, they are in the spotlight in movies, television series, comics, cartoons, anime, and books. We love them, and in a way, fact has inspired fiction in ways no one in the 1800's could ever imagine. Those few brave writers who wrote about the vampires and tried to educate people (This is consumption. Vampires are simply innocents accused of something supernatural, etc.) should know their message was heard. The terrifying thing here is to imagine how the misinformation about pandemics gave birth to this. With no means to double-check if someone was dead or alive, I imagine coming back from the grave happened quite a lot! Still, we haven't forgotten our roots or our imagination.

REFERENCES

1. Etymology of the word "vampire"–https://www.etymonline.com/word/vampire
2. FORUM: Word Reference Discussion on Ubyr – Etymology–https://forum.wordreference.com/threads/vampire-ubyr-etymology.2615925/
3. 'Genesis of the word "Vampire"' by Vampriologist–http://vampirologist.blogspot.com/2009/01/genesis-of-word-vampire.html
4. Vampire folklore by region–https://en.wikipedia.org/wiki/Vampire_folklore_by_region
5. Etymology of the word "Strigoi"–https://en.wiktionary.org/wiki/strigoi
6. Podcast – *Lore* episode 72 'A Grave Mistake'–http://www.lorepodcast.com/episodes/72
7. Strigoi–https://en.wikipedia.org/wiki/Strigoi
8. Bible, New King James Version–https://biblia.com/books/nkjv/Re17.6
9. "How Old is the Bible" by Paul Ratner–http://bigthink.com/paul-ratner/how-old-is-the-bible
10. The Sibylline Oracles–http://www.sacred-texts.com/cla/sib/sib.pdf
11. The Oracle: Real or Myth?–http://www.scififantasynetwork.com/oracle-real-myth/
12. *Vikram and the Vampire* by Sir Richard F. Burton–https://www.gutenberg.org/files/2400/2400-h/2400-h.htm
13. Sanskrit–https://en.wikipedia.org/wiki/Sanskrit
14. Baital Pachisi–https://en.wikipedia.org/wiki/Baital_Pachisi
15. *The Baital Pachisi* English Translation by WB Barker–https://archive.org/details/TheBaitalPachisiEnglishTranslationWBBarker1855
16. Pishacha–https://en.wikipedia.org/wiki/Pishacha
17. *The Book of Were-wolves* by Sabine Baring-Gould–http://www.gutenberg.org/ebooks/5324
18. Moroi–https://en.wikipedia.org/wiki/Moroi
19. *Vampyrismus* by Freiherr van Gerard Swieten, 1700-1772–http://www.gutenberg.org/files/30886/30886-h/30886-h.htm
20. *Russian Fairy Tales: A Choice Collection of Muscovite Folk-lore* by Ralston, 1828-1889, Published 1872–http://www.gutenberg.org/files/22373/22373-h/22373-h.htm#Page_295
21. *The Vampyre; a Tale* by John William Polidori, 1795-1821, Published in April 1819 issue of New Monthly Magazine and was there erroneously attributed to Lord Byron, Fiction – Vampire – http://www.gutenberg.org/files/6087/6087-h/6087-h.htm
22. *Carmilla* by Joseph Sheridan Le Fanu, 1814-1873, Fiction–Vampire – http://www.gutenberg.org/files/10007/10007-h/10007-h.htm
23. Vampires in Russia–https://encyclopedia2.thefreedictionary.com/Russia%2C+Vampires+in
24. Bathory's Torturous Escapades are Exposed–https://www.history.com/this-day-in-history/bathorys-torturous-escapades-are-exposed
25. "High Albania" by Mary Edith Durham–http://www.digital.library.upenn.edu/women/durham/albania/albania-IV.html
26. *Vampyrism* by Gerard van Swieten 1768–http://www.gutenberg.org/files/30886/30886-0.txt
27. How Mosquitos Came To Be – A Tlingit Legend–http://www.firstpeople.us/FP-Html-Legends/How_Mosquitoes_Came_To_Be-Tlingit.html
28. *Lore: Monstrous Creatures* by Aaron Mahnke–https://www.amazon.com/World-Lore-Monstrous-Creatures-ebook/dp/B0738LH55P
29. The Real Dracula: Vlad the Impaler–https://www.livescience.com/40843-real-dracula-vlad-the-impaler.html
30. Gilles de Rais – Medieval Vampire–https://www.vampires.com/gilles-de-rais-medieval-vampire/
31. 'History of Vampires' Recounts Woodstock Tale–https://www.thevermontstandard.com/2010/11/%E2%80%98history-of-vampires%E2%80%99-recounts-woodstock-tale/
32. *Dracula* by Bram Stoker–http://www.gutenberg.org/files/345/345-h/345-h.htm
33. *The Golden Bough* by James George Frazer–https://ia800303.us.archive.org/3/items/cu31924021569128/cu31924021569128.pdf

21 WINTER MYTHOLOGICAL FIGURES YOU DIDN'T KNOW

VALERIE WILLIS

When we think of the holiday season, we are often swamped with the modern rush of shopping, gifts, and pulling families and friends together. Let's take a step back to a time when what mattered was recognizing "winter is coming" and the huge need to prepare for the Winter Solstice, Yuletide festivals, winter rituals and, more importantly, receive the entities of old. After revisiting my favorite resources, this is my collection of 21 winter mythological figures you didn't know. Some may surprise you with their strong archaeological connections, poetic and musical associations, and inspirations or crossover into recognizable pop-culture content. Pay careful attention to how nature, the flow of the sun especially at the peak of winter, plays huge roles in many of these.

ALCYOONE

GREEK

Alcyoone is a goddess who throws herself into the waves when her lover washes up on shore, so she can join him in death. She is reborn as a Kingfisher, and in some accounts so is her lover. During two weeks in winter, she nests and hatches her young. It is said these are the only two weeks where the seas remain calm during the colder months.

AMATERASU

JAPANESE

Amaterasu rules over the heavens until her brother, Susanowa, challenges her. The winner will be the new ruler of the kingdom of heaven. Amaterasu accepts, taking Susanowa's sword, chewing it up and spitting out in the form of three female deities. He in turn takes her five-strand necklace, chews it up, and spits forth five male deities, winning the contest. Distraught, the sun goddess hides away in a cave, and thus winter comes to the land. Eighty myriad gods try to lure her out of the cave with a large celebration and party. In the end, it takes a gift of a mirror called Kagami and Uzume, her daughter, dancing to cheer her up, making her laugh. She comes out, putting everything back in order again.

BALDER/BALDUR
NORSE

Baldur dreams of his own death, and his mother, Frigga, begs nature not to harm him. Unfortunately, she overlooks the humble mistletoe (which Loki notes). Baldur's blind twin brother, Hodr, is given a spear made of mistletoe, or in some accounts a sword tempered by mistletoe named Mistelltein, and Loki has the two fight. Hodr strikes down Baldur, killing him. His wife Nanna dies of grief, and they are laid side-by-side on the funeral pyre. Odin leans in, whispers "Rebirth," and thus he is born again. Another story says Hela would not free Baldur from Niflheim until every creature sheds a tear for him. A giantess said to be Loki in disguise does not and thus Baldur is stuck. Frigga declares the mistletoe a symbol of love, thus countering the element of death.

BALOR OF THE EVIL EYE
PRE-CELTIC

Balor is known as the king of Fomorians who invaded and ruled Ireland for some time before the Celts. He has a third eye in the middle of his forehead which could spit fire and destruction. At one point, he steals a magical cow from a Celtic hero Cian, leading to a prophecy of his own grandson bringing about his death. As for his association with winter, his bitter nature is to blame for smiting the growth of plants with frost and chill. Balor is also a god of the Underworld.

BOAND/BOANN
IRISH

Boand is the woman of white cows, or shining cow, or the Cow Goddess. She also gave up her name to the river Boyne. The story says she found a well, lifted the rock blocking the spring to give life to the land, and the river poured forth, drowning her. The one-eyed salmon, Fintan, is believed to be a symbol of her inner-vision and outer-blindness. During June, drinking from this river gives you the talent of a seer and poet. In fact, one of the most known winter solstice sites, *Bru Na Bionne* or "Palace of Boann" is said to be the location where the good god Dagda lures her from her husband, Nechtan. Here Dagda froze the sky for nine months, so she could give birth to their child, and Nechtan was none the wiser for it seemed only a day had passed.

BONA DEA
ROMAN, GREEK, CELTIC

Roman women gather in early December at a secret temple on Aventine Hill in Rome to hold an ancient ritual. They all come to worship the fertility goddess Bona Dea. Only women are allowed and more importantly, all are forbidden to talk about men or anything masculine. The interesting note is this ritual is said to be from a more ancient religion. Snakes are associated with it in conjunction to a tale about the goddess having been raped by her father in serpent form. Others have found connection to Fuana,

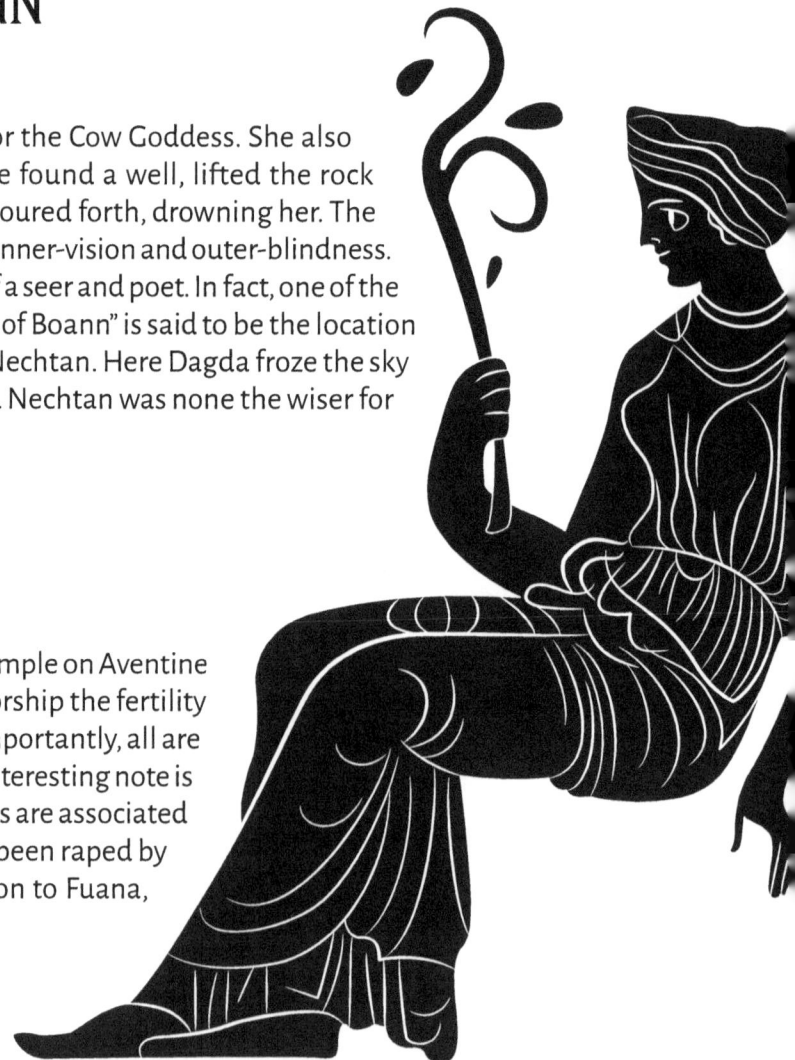

Maia, and Ops, which are Celtic and Greek deities. In my own work, this connects to my character Nemaine, one of three Celtic sorceress sisters from The Cedric Series.

CAILLEACH BHEUR

PRE-CELTIC, GAELIC, SCOTTISH, BRITISH, ARTHURIAN

Her name means *veiled one* or *hooded one*, which in terms of the older myths meant *aged* or *burdened* in some fashion. Other names tied into this deity included Beira, Queen of Winter, the Triple Goddess, Mother of Magic, and a creation goddess of old. She is known most famously for flipping between an old hag and young maiden. Most active during the dark days between Samhain (Oct 31) and Beltaine (May 1), she arrives in late fall, bringing storms and causing the earth to die, a witch-god who turns to stone on Beltaine only to be revived again.

As an old woman, she has one eye in the middle of her face, bad teeth, a blue-gray face, uncanny eyesight reaching up to 20 miles (as if seeing the back of her hand), and matted hair. In some tales, she is called the Hag of Hair or Hag of the Long Teeth and chokes hunters who kill pregnant animals in the wild woods. Another aspect says she carries materials in a basket or her apron to mold the land. She is to blame for the rocky landscape, dropping rocks from her basket or apron or throwing them at men in anger. There are tales of King Authur's contenders asked to kiss or have intercourse with an old hag. Any brave enough to do so soon discover her to be a splendid young woman who bestows sovereignty on any man kind enough to oblige an old woman.

Going back to her older, Pre-Celtic roots, Bheur is part of a cosmic tale with no name for her original believers. She is the winter sun's daughter, born old and growing younger throughout winter, ending the season as a young spring maiden. Scottish beliefs depict her as a crane with sticks in her beak to forecast storms or a herd of deer. During winter storms, a common proverb is "The Cailleach is trampling the blankets tonight" and refer as the "sharp old wife" or Daughter of the little sun, winter sun." They believe the Mumming dances, celebratory sword dances with a wooden stick, drive her away, which has inspired songs during this festive tradition. One song known more recently is "The Mummer's Dance" by Loreena McKennitt (https://www.youtube.com/watch?v=LzE32ChEp24).

DEMETER

GREEK

A well-earned title for Demeter is *Dark Mother of Winter* and for many reasons. First off, she is just as famous as Hera in terms of her temper. In more than one account, she turns people into lizards when they dare joke about her or her children. There is even a tale of Tantalus feeding her his son Pelops, in which she happily eats his shoulder and replaces it with an ivory one when the gods reassemble the boy. When Hades takes her daughter Persephone to the underworld, Demeter grieves for her. At first, she travels the earth looking for clues as an old hag. Soon, she encounters a kindhearted king who lets her in his household, and she becomes a wet-nurse for his son. Demeter loves the boy so much, she wants him to become immortal, so she throws him into the fireplace. Naturally, the Queen kicks her out, and Demeter continues to grieve for her daughter, killing the earth. Her dark, cold onslaught ends when her daughter is given leave to visit. Thus, Demeter is credited with the changing seasons.

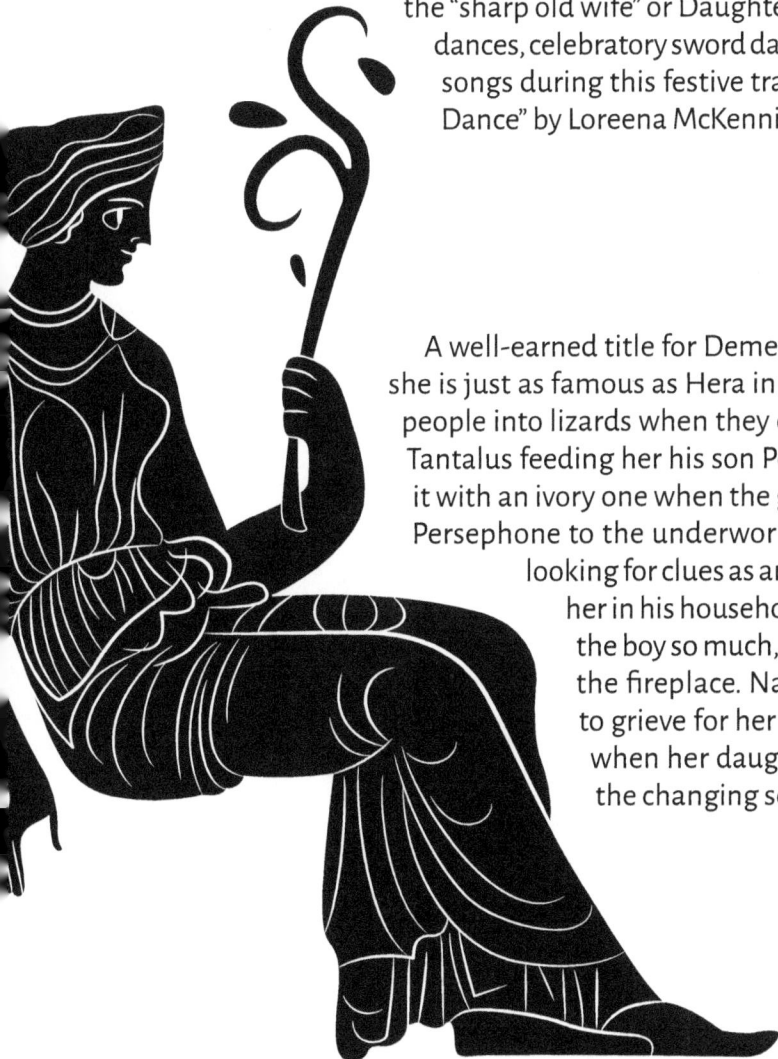

ESTONEA-PESTA
NORTH AMERICA

Known as the *Lord of Cold Weather*, he provides protection to Sacred Otter by giving him a Snow-lodge. Thus, he is responsible for shelter and protection from the cold which he oversees, making him one of the few positive winter time deities.

FRIGGA/FRAU HOLLE/FREYA/MOTHER HULDA
GERMANIC, NORSE, SCANDINAVIAN

We all know Frigga is responsible for labeling the mistletoe a symbol of love due to Baldur's death. She is also associated with the evergreen plants often used to symbolize the Yule season. Another story says snow falls because she is shaking out her feathery mattress. You can even find a story in the Grimm's fairytales called "Mother Hulda" capturing this fun notion.

> *"You must take great pains to make my bed well, and shake it up thoroughly, so that the feathers fly about, and then in the world it snows, for I am Mother Hulda."*
> *Grimm's Complete Fairy Tales*

FREY, LORD OF ALFA OR ELVES
NORSE & SCANDINAVIAN

Frey, a better-known entity, is known as the *Lord of Elves*, twin brother of Freya, but the ritual in tribute to his elves is during winter. An *alfablot* is a ritual or sacrifice made by humans, normally performed by the women of the household. There are seasonal prerequisites involved and many blessings call for inspiration, prayer, and even storytelling during the ritual itself. Offerings are in the form of food and art. Frey holds great importance in acknowledging many of the Norse gods and their roles with the elves, including Thor and Freya.

GILLIAN/JILLIAN
BRITISH FOLKLORE, ARTHURIAN

This spring maiden or goddess is imprisoned in a maze or labyrinth. When this happens, winter starts to fall upon the land. When she finally escapes, springtime can begin again. The culprit is often unclear, but sometimes it's her suitors trying to hide her away from one another. Gillian's tale has inspired some festival events that play out this scenario: a girl finding her way out of a turf maze of sorts.

Gwynn ap Nudd/Herne the Hunter/Gabriel

Welsh Hero, British

He is the Welsh king of Fairyland known as the *White one, son of the Dark* who rules over beautiful tiny people in blue. They ance all night, but he leads the Wild Hunt when they raid the land of the living or mortals. He competes for the spring maiden's hand in marriage, but is defeated, thus ending winter. There is a belief he still roams the Windsor Forest in England, where he disappears at midnight. He is also famous for keeping vicious fairy hounds.

Hoder/Hodr/Hod

Norse

The blind twin brother to Baldur, he is known as the *God of Darkness and Winter*. After killing his brother, he sets off Ragnarok, the destruction of the world, thanks to Loki's trickery. This is the mythological equivalent to a nuclear winter happening after Hodr drops the mistletoe bomb.

Holly King

Celtic, Welsh, Arthurian, British

There is a story about forest gods, similar to the Green Knight in tales involving King Arthur, battling for supremacy. The Oak King and the Holly King duke it out, causing the onslaught of fall and winter. At the winter solstice, the Holly King is defeated, and the Oak King brings back spring and summer. Oddly enough, a song dating to the Medieval period is inspired by this tale, called "The Holly and The Ivy" as made famous by the late Natalie Cole (https://www.youtube.com/watch?v=_HtMWopE-zQ). The holly is a symbol of masculinity while the ivy is its feminine counterpart.

> *The holly and the ivy,*
> *When they are both full grown,*
> *Of all the trees that are in the wood,*
> *The holly bears the crown.*
>
> Lyrics for *"The Holly and The Ivy"*

Hrimgrimnir

Norse

Hrimgrimnir is a rime-giant, or main giant, invoked by the fertility god Skirnir in an effort to help his master Frey, Lord of Elves, force Gerda, the giantess, to marry him. He is among the first giants in Norse mythology, representing the strong forces of nature in the form of the cold northern winter. Gerda is told if she does not marry Frey, she will be Hrimgrimnir's mate and live out her days in Hel, the underworld. He aligns with the changing of the seasons, eternal night, and the dangers of the cold.

POOKA OF KILDARE/PHOOKA
PRE-CELTIC, IRISH FOLKLORE, BRITISH, WELSH, NORSE

Pookas are a strange hobgoblin who can take the form of a donkey, white horse, black dog, a calf, a goat, or any combination of these. For the most part, *pookas* are mischievous, but occasionally have been known to aid farmers in their work. The Pooka of Kildare comes to a young boy's rescue when he tries to support the household farm. He refuses any gifts of gratitude, but the boy insists, giving him clothes. He disappears after that. Other tales say he is to blame for blighting plants, people falling over during the winter season, or attacks increasing after Samhain (Oct 31). Some stories say he comes up out of the ground, between your legs, taking you for a ride or simply knocking you into the mud. At Castle Pooka in Doneraile, the poet Edmund Spenser insisted one was haunting him.

SKADI/SKAOI/SKADE
NORSE

Famous for being a cold-hearted giantess and goddess, she represents winter, skiers, and hunters. Only two people could touch her with their warmth: Njord her husband and the god of summer along with Loki (often represented by the fire's hearth). Ironically enough, Skade picks her husband by lining them up with only their feet exposed and picks the most alluring pair. She is both shocked and unhappy about the result, since Njord and she never get along, neither willing to visit the other's palaces.

SPIDER WOMAN & THE HAWK MAIDEN
NORTH AMERICAN

Soyal celebrates the winter solstice to celebrate the sun's victory over the darkness of winter, specifically the Spider Woman, who helps reclaim the wife of the Son of Light, and the Hawk Maiden, who aids in their escape with flight. This celebration draws in the Kachine, or ancestral spirits, who only walk the land during winter and return underground during summer.

ULLER/ULL
NORSE, SCANDINAVIAN

The male counterpart to Skade, Ull is the god of skiers and hunting. Often depicted with snowshoes, bow, and shield, his imagery, especially the bone nature of the snowshoes, reaches far into Scandinavian beliefs. Poetry suggests he uses the shield as a boat while others label him a clever and cunning magician who travels overseas.

YUKKI-ONA/SNOW WOMAN/LADY OF THE SNOW
JAPANESE

Yukki-ona is an evil female spirit who died in the snow or was a woman left in poverty by her husband. In one story, a master and his pupil encounter one of these phantoms. She uses her icy breath and freezes the master, allowing the younger man to escape. Later, married, he realizes his wife is the Snow Woman from before, and she simply disappears in a cold mist of air.

WORDS FROM THE AUTHOR

Most of these deities come mainly from Nordic and Celtic roots because that is where most of my research for my own fantasy romance series comes from, and secondly, their cold region plays a huge part in the amount of cold, snow, winter, and darkness-based deities. Often these stories explain the shortest day of the year, while others serve as a warning, at times bluntly to say, "the cold can kill you." Snow is pretty, but like the Snow Woman, her breath can freeze you to death. In other stories, they reveal spring cannot come into being without winter giving birth to it first as it hints in Cailleach Bheur's story. This article was inspired by a manga, or comic, and recent anime, cartoon, called *Ancient Magus Bride* by Kore Yamazaki that included many Celtic deities of old in her winter chapters (Chapter 25 was most intriguing). It brought great joy and excitement to see some forgotten entities brought to life in her artwork and storytelling. Happy holidays, and beware of the northern winds and freezing snow!

REFERENCES

1. *Deities of the Winter Solstice* by Patti Wigington–https://www.thoughtco.com/deities-of-the-winter-solstice-2562976
2. Deities and Personifications of Seasons on Wikipedia–https://en.wikipedia.org/wiki/Deities_and_personifications_of_seasons
3. *The Dictionary of Mythology* by JA Coleman
4. *The Encyclopedia of Celtic Mythology and Folklore* by Patricia Monaghan
5. *Norse Mythology A to Z* Third Edition, by Kathleen N Daly, revised by Marlan Rengel
6. "The Mummer's Dance" sung by Loreena McKennitt–https://www.youtube.com/watch?v=L-zE32ChEp24
7. "The Holly & The Ivy" sung by Natalie Cole–https://www.youtube.com/watch?v=_HtM-WopE-zQ
8. Alfablot Ritual written by Paradox, Raven and Shamrock at ADF.org–https://www.adf.org/rituals/norse/gleichentag/alfablot.html
9. Bru na Bionne Visitor Site–http://www.ireland.com/en-us/what-is-available/attractions-built-heritage/museums-and-attractions/destinations/republic-of-ireland/meath/donore/all/1-12303/?gclid=Cj0KCQiAl8rQBRDrARIsAEW_To9uZWL95DR1Mm_i4RioiSjtmirC-ClQmJrYOyibPEPiLeLTp3DpZ9_8aAlRJEALw_wcB&gclsrc=aw.ds
10. Mumming – A Yuletide tradition–http://www.irishcultureandcustoms.com/ACalend/Mummers.html
11. Aventine Keyhole–https://www.atlasobscura.com/places/the-aventine-keyhole-rome
12. *Grimm's Complete Fairy Tales* – Barnes & Noble 1993 edition

www.ingramcontent.com/pod-product-compliance
Lightning Source LLC
Chambersburg PA
CBHW042353030426
42336CB00029B/3469